The Power of Politics in the Governance of the Poor in India

About the Author

Dr. Margaret Khalakdina is an independent consultant in Human Development. She did her Masters and Ph.D. at Syracuse University and Cornell University respectively.

She has been the Dean at the College of Home Science, Haryana Agricultural University, Hissar. She was also Executive Director of the Indian Council for Child Welfare.

She has worked for UNICEF in African countries and has been a consultant to WHO and FAO in Egypt and Uganda.

She has written books and articles on early childcare, human development and human ecology, besides contributing to seminars and discussions on topics relating to human development.

The Power of Politics in the Governance of the Poor in India

M. Khalakdina

CONCEPT PUBLISHING COMPANY PVT. LTD.
NEW DELHI-110059

ISBN-13: 978-81-8069-994-8

First Published 2013

Published and Printed by

Concept Since 1974

Concept Publishing Company Pvt. Ltd.
A/15-16, Commercial Block, Mohan Garden
New Delhi-110059 (India)
T: 25351460, 25351794, *F*: 091-11-25357109
E: publishing@conceptpub.com, W: www.conceptpub.com
Editorial Office: H-13, Bali Nagar, New Delhi-110 015, India.

Cataloging in Publication Data--*Courtesy:* D.K. Agencies (P) Ltd. <docinfo@dkagencies.com>

Khalakdina, Margaret.
The power of politics in the governance of the poor in India / M. Khalakdina.
p. cm.
Includes bibliographical references and index.
ISBN 9788180699948

1. Poor—India—Social conditions. 2. Poor—Government policy—India. 3. India—Population—Economic aspects. I. Title.

DDC 339.460954 23

To the Child of the Poor Urban Mother

A babe whimpered under the eluding shade of a banyan tree
Her sister tugging back and forth a piece of rope
That hung a fragile knot to the humble hammock
Wishing she was free like the bird on spree.
A little boy made a castle of broken bricks, red
While in the distance toiling figures moved in a silhouette
Carrying, moving, bending, like puppets in a scene set.
Dust swirled and whirled, flies settled gently
A little one paddled with not a clothing shred
In the coffee coloured mud of a rain rivulet
That spilt all matters of rubbish as it sped.
The tin roof clattered, the plastic covers flew
And the damp wood refused its fire to brew.
The mother lifted the sleeping cherub and said,
"Hush little one, you will be cared for and safe
Till I return from my toil that began at day break.

Preface

This book aims to provide the reader with a narrative of the conditions of the poor in India over a period of time since Independence. The attempt is to picturise the Government's efforts in working for the provision of essentials for the poor.

We know very little of the conditions of the poor spread over geographical areas during the time of the pre-colonial and colonial eras. It was when the British overthrew the last Moghul King, Bahadur Shah Zafar, and proclaimed themselves as the rulers that the poor came to know about the *ferangies* taking over their territories. During their rule which came to be known as the British Raj, as we all know, there was little attention paid to the poor. As it is well known from history the British paid little attention to the development and welfare of the Indian people in general. The Raj was more interested in the collection of revenues and taxes and finding ways to augmenting its coffers through the provision of railways to carry goods and a system of education for the middle and upper middle classes in India with whom they could communicate. The common masses of India were disconnected from the rulers and the miniscule number of rich Indians, most of whom were the *Rajas* or *Nawabs* of little states and their appendages, were beholden to the Britishers. During the freedom movement of India, the English-educated leaders like Pandit Jawaharlal Nehru and Sardar Patel took upon themselves to fight against the Britishers by using the principle of *swaraj* and *ahimsa* as propounded by Gandhi at that time.

After Independence, the Indian national leaders set up a Constitution which the principles of democracy, namely, Equality, Justice and Fraternity. From hindsight, it is evident that the principles of democracy were little understood by most of the people of India who were uneducated and, in any case, were not homogeneous in their perception of what the new system of political governance meant. They had been under the yoke of feudalism for a long time. They only understood that there were the rich who were their masters and that they were their servants. To the poor, the meaning of the new system was tangential since not much had changed in their life and they continued to live under the same conditions as before.

The newly constituted Government of independent India and its leaders were aware of the need for and enthusiastic about bringing about the betterment of the lives of those who were downtrodden. Therefore, the first attempt of the new Government was to build Plans for a successive period of five years within which there were detailed developmental plans. The initial Plans naturally turned towards improvement of agriculture so as to ensure food security for people, since the majority in the rural areas were poor. The Government developed programmes like the community development programmes and programmes for making the country self-sufficient in food and employment generation. Following on, small-scale industrial development was also the focus.

We must consider, however, that even those who governed little understood the operational definitions of the high-sounding words of the constitutional directives. There was not much education among them, nor an understanding of how Equality, Justice and Fraternity would be implemented majority who were poor, in as much as the later lived a subsistence-level existence. Further there was much heterogeneity, especially in terms of caste, ethnicity, differential regional areas, differential language, and there was inadequate infrastructure and therefore lack of communication between different areas. To some degree communication and infrastructure still suffer even after more than sixty years of Independence and planned developmental efforts.

The following pages present a historical narrative of the various programmes and their effects on the poor. As of today, India still suffers from many negatively toned indicators such as continuing lack of basic necessities for the poor. However, this book does not attempt to deal with them in detail as they are many and much deep-rooted. This book attempts to show in some small measure as to how the poor are neglected not by Constitutional directives but by the interpretation and implementation by those who form the polity.

It is well-known that power makes one more deeply intense on gaining more power and, over the years, the aggregation of power to the powerful in the polity has in many ways blurred their vision of the uplift of the poor who form the majority of Indians. To this day, the plight of the poor has not been successfully attended to, inspite of pledges and promises of the political parties that governed India. The theme, therefore, of this book is that, for generations the poor were poor and as we foresee it they will continue to be poor in future unless there is some upheaval to instill in the coming generations a sense of genuine commitment and transparency of policies to really focus ethically on the poor. As is apparent in this the 21st century, the picture is dismal and it will be a long time before the poor have some sense of equality and some measure of justice meted out to them in the same way that is being done for the miniscule rich upper socio-economic classes.

This book is a straightforward communication with the reader, setting a scenario as the author sees it. It contains thoughts that often pass through a common man's mind as he struggles to survive, especially in the context of the rising cost of living inspite of the glowing reports that India is a progressively emerging developing country with a high GDP growth rate. We do not see the effect of the GDP growth in the improvement of the status of the poor. We do not see the improvement in the life of the struggling rickshaw man, or the poor farmer who tills his little infertile land, or the casual labourer in market places hoping that some *thekedaar* would employ him to whom he would be grateful and readily give a part of his earnings as commission.

There have been protests and a rise of voices in terms of demanding from the Government as to why the governance is unable to bring the developmental benefits to the common man, why the governance is riddled with inefficiency and corruption, why the Commonwealth Games flyovers have been poorly constructed, why housing apartments meant for the average man are being allotted to friends of friends and relatives of relatives of those who wield power. Where does the wealth created by the modern technology go? Where does even the "trickle" of it go? This voice is being raised by the rising middle class who are becoming aware of the disjointedness between the stated policies of the government and their implementation. They are appalled at the different types of corruption that are mounting almost one on top of the other.

This book is meant to urge people to give serious thought to the issues of good governance and to add to their awareness of the dismal prevailing conditions, especially of the poor. For instance, why should there be so many child deaths in a West Bengal hospital as have occurred recently? And, again, why should there be malnourished children with large stomachs, discoloured hair and puny hands stretched sitting along road-sides waiting for money to be thrown at them? This book is especially meant for the young and upcoming generation who will be the leaders of the future. Governance is meant for everyone and not just for those who grab what they can before it reaches the target group. Much can be said, but the little that is said in this book is meant to touch those who are concerned and proud of their country. We often listen to the comments from other countries that India is a country of the poor, dusty, dirty and filled with ragamuffins, beggars, people who cheat, so that one has to bargain to get the right price. This scenario pictured to the outside world of the poor state of affairs in our country is of our own making, for, while lofty principles and policies are in place, their mismanagement by unethical controllers is what robs the country of its dignity. Whatever development efforts have been made in India have not been successful in reaching the poor segments of society to the extent possible.

The use of power occurs in every nation, group or community. It is only the degree that differs. In some it is extensive and in others it is less so. The world is becoming so telescoped through the electronic media that information circulates very quickly from one to another in no time. The unhealthy wielding of power is in the very nature of the human being, given the opportunity to do so in a covert manner. With the use of spy cameras, phone-tapping and the quick hacking of computer information of others, it is getting easier by the day to know what is happening in the lives of others.

It stands to reason that the more developed a country's technology, the greater is its power to gain control over those who are relatively less technologically oriented. It is a tendency of the more powerful countries to have a hold over the less powerful countries in the global arena. This same phenomenon of the hold of the powerful over the powerless is very vivid in India. This occurs when the more powerful want to aggrandize more territories and wealth. Rich countries, for example, will continue to sell arms to poorer countries, because they are produced in prolific numbers and these rich countries want to hold sway over the less rich countries. In like manner, the rich in India want to hold sway over the poor. Well-known international events are the sale of arms, the existence of drug cartels, and the famous system of cutting of aid to poor countries and laying down injunctions through sanctions.

India, however, has gone through the period of being beholden to such rich countries. Now it is fairly well-industrialised and food production is fairly well-developed. Yet, we can see how disadvantaged many of its people are, especially the poor.

India has a high MMR and IMR rate especially among the poor for whom the polity has claimed that they made provisions for taking care of these problems. It is not that India does not have resources. In fact many of its resources are untapped and yet to be converted into revenues for the health and welfare of the poor. In real terms, India has much untapped wealth in its mineral resources, in its ability to provide alternative sources of energy and in increasing accessibility and ability to communicate with the poor. Unfortunately, what are being discussed and decided by the law-makers of India in the Parliament hardly affect the lives of the poor as these decisions are not put into action when they relate to raising the living conditions of the poor. Words and actions do not tally for the majority of the Indians who look upon the Government in assisting them in raising their livelihood. It is to be remembered that the Constitution is said to have been set up "For the People", "By the People". This necessarily implies the inclusion of the majority, namely, the poor. However, this is not evident. Unfortunately, the high-sounding principles of the constitution do not seem to apply to the poor. For, in actual fact the concentration is not for the people but only for a segment of the people, not by the people but by a few people who hold political power and not of the people as its radial focus is spread only to the rich and the powerful.

When these powerful groups hold the poor under their control and do not attempt to fulfill their needs, it becomes an ironical situation since it is these very poor who have voted them into power. The people in power tend to become evasive, seek delays and make excuses for not fulfilling their responsibilities. It is only at the time of elections when they appeal for votes that they put on the garb of saints and institute strategies that indicate a government that has a façade with the double meaning, one that is shown to the people and the one that is practised covertly for their own benefit.

It is within this context that we attempt here to discuss the type of governance the Indian majority is subjected to. This majority is the most fragile, the most disadvantaged and the most powerless: namely, the poor. By writing this narrative of the historical political meandering it is hoped that it will create greater public awareness of the plight of the poor.

Acknowledgements

This is to acknowledge the sincerity, dedication and the hard work of Mr. Shaji without whose assistance and cooperation this book would have been difficult to complete. I thank him. My gratitude also goes to Mrs. Shakuntala Dixit who assisted me in the referencing and editing of this book. I am also grateful to several others of my friends and colleagues who have given me their time.

M. Khalakdina

Contents

1

Poverty: Its Meaning and Implications

There are various interpretations of the term "poverty". This term relates to a package of variables adversely affecting the life of the majority in India. The most general understanding of poverty deals with the availability of food to eat, a shelter to live in and minimum clothes to wear. But, there are also psychological aspects of poverty. Poor people experience lack of a powerful effective voice and freedom to act within the limits of liberty and fraternity. They perceive themselves, consciously or unconsciously, as exploited and experience humiliation in many walks of life, as they are subjected to indignities in their interaction with the better off. Thus, poverty is a complex, multidimensional phenomenon. The World Bank defines poverty as "*an unacceptable human deprivation in terms of economic opportunity, education, health and nutrition, as well as lack of empowerment and security*" (World Bank, 2001) Sinha has stated that "poverty and illiteracy together tend to cause uncertainty and fear of scarcity" which is called the "poverty syndrome" by him (Sinha, J.B.P., 1977).

Apparently both qualitative and quantitative assessments are necessary to view poverty status in terms of its total parameters.

With the introduction of the policies of "liberalization" and "globalization", India is said to have experienced a high and vigorous economic growth, but by contrast and ironically so, the largest proportion of its population are still poor without having a decent standard of living. This large disadvantaged group in India is in high contrast to the miniscule well-to-do. The "poor" lack skills, abilities and opportunities to raise their economic and social status in relation to the better off.

Poverty is a relative term depending upon whose perception it is. For example, a bus-driver may consider that he is poor in relation to the driver of a BMW that stops with his bus at the stop sign. The laborer who gets on to his bus considers he is poorer than the bus driver, while the rich man in the BMW considers he is poorer than his counterpart working in the corporate world with him.

Furthermore, poverty varies considerably among nations. For example, rich nations generally have different levels of understanding of poverty than do the poor nations. It is difficult for those living in a developed country of the West to truly perceive and understand the level of poverty in India. In India, poverty means precisely lack of essentials. In the West, even those who are perceived as being "poor" can live in well-constructed dwellings, with heating, clean running water, indoor ablution facilities and even possess vehicles, however rundown they may be. Such facilities are luxuries for the poor in India. They perceive that such amenities are available only among the rich in India as in the Western world. This little information they know mainly through the social media. Governance is such that in America a jobless man can claim social benefits unlike in India and definitely not with the poor. In India, there is no such subsidy as pension for the poor or social security for the unemployed. In India, a common man who is not in a pension-paying regular job find it difficult to pay for medical expenses, whereas in the United States, healthcare is uniformly available to those who go through the portals of emergency care in hospitals. In other western countries, healthcare is supported by the state health services, as in the UK. In the West, there are soup kitchens for the hungry, shelter homes for those who are living off the streets and "food stamps" for the poor. By comparison, these facilities do not exist for the poor in India. There are no beggars in the West but in India they abound the urban cities. Thus, the term poverty connotes different conceptualizations among peoples of different nationalities. It then follows that the term "poverty" denotes a situational phenomenon differentiating the poor from the non-poor.

In the larger sense, poverty means essentially "lack of", which means lacuna in certain areas of well-being. There are concepts like "poverty of mind", implying lack of intelligence, and "social poverty", implying lack of interaction with the group or community in which the person lives. However, more directly, poverty denotes "lack of" economic wealth, whether in the form of money, property or territory. While discussing the term "poverty", we wish to refer to both economic and social poverty simultaneously as, in the context of the Indian social fabric, they are intertwined.

Sociologically speaking, India's population is divided into what are called socio-economic classes which are as follows: the "upper", the "middle" and the "lower". In the past, all visitors to India invariably noted that the "lower classes" formed the bulk of India's population and they belonged to various occupational groups, namely, different artisans from basket and rope makers to cloth-printers, embroiders, carpet makers, silk-weavers, blacksmiths, tin workers, carpenters, oil-men, barbers, jugglers, mountebanks, street singers, brewers, tailors, betel leaf sellers, flower sellers, masons, stone-cutters, bullock-cart drivers, *doli*-carriers, water-carriers, domestic servants, *dhobis* and workers in a hundred other simple skilled and unskilled crafts. However, the major proportion of the "lower classes" is agricultural labourers in rural areas and casual labourers in urban areas, especially at construction sites. (K. M. Ashraf, 2000)

A significant proportion of India's population cannot be fitted into any of the above social class categories because they suffer from acute and chronic poverty. They are also called "the deprived", meaning deprived of necessities for a basic living. Geo-ecologically, most of them live in rural, tribal and far-off settlement areas. They are largely illiterate, do not have remunerative skills and lack a world vision, living in their own parochial parameters.

A crucial necessity for basic living is food and its nutrition. 2011 Global Hunger Index (GHI) Report ranked India 15th. India's GHI between 1996 and 2011 went up from 22.9 to 23.7 while its neighbouring countries of Pakistan, Nepal, and Bangladesh succeeded in improving hunger condition. Levels of malnutrition in India are exceptionally high even when compared to the poorest countries of the sub-Saharan Africa. It is said that about 46 per cent of India's children under the age of three are underweight (due to under-nourishment) (International Institute for Population Sciences (IPS) and Macro International, 2007) compared to 28 per cent in sub-Saharan Africa and only 8 per cent in China (India

Health News, 2007). India has the highest proportion of malnourished women among the developing countries. 70 per cent of the non-pregnant and 75 per cent of the pregnant women in India are said to be malnutritioned in terms of iron-deficiency (Mason, John, Adams Bailes, Mary Beda-Andourou, Nancy Copeland, Teresa Curtis, Megan Deitchler, Leigh Foster, Marianna Hensley, Peter Horjus, Christine Johnson, Tina Lloren, Anna Memdez, Mary Munoz, Jonathan Rivers and Gwyneth Vance 2005.

India's official poverty measure has long been based upon the ability to purchase a minimum recommended daily diet of 2,400 kilocalories (kcal) in rural areas and 2,100 kcal in urban areas. Rural areas are usually presumed to have higher calorie requirements because of greater physical activity among rural residents. India's Planning Commission in 1973-74 estimated that a monthly per capita consumption expenditure of Rs. 49 in rural areas and Rs. 57 in urban areas would suffice to purchase the food items required to satisfy the above-prescribed calorie requirements. In the subsequent years, these cut-off figures of monthly consumption expenditure were revised taking into account the price rise index. Accordingly, these figures calculated by the Planning Commission for 2010 were Rs. 356 per person in rural areas and Rs. 539 in urban areas per month (Govt. of India, 2009). In these poverty estimates, factors such as housing, health care, and transportation are not taken into account. About 40 per cent of Indian families live in one-room houses. 39 per cent of all married couples in India do not have an independent room to themselves. There are more places of worship in the country than schools, colleges and hospitals combined (Saran, R., 2003).

Economic disparity exists at all levels: at the global level among nations of the world and within nations among different ethnic, religious, regional and other social groups. Economic disparity among nations is perhaps the root cause of upheavals and warfare in the global world. For example, the Western countries, and perhaps Japan, have one of the highest indices of economic wealth which is reflected in their technological power, in their industrialisation, transport systems, communication technology and other infrastructures. Many of the economically under-developed countries in Asia and Africa perceive that the developed countries of the West make efforts to take away the resources of the under-developed countries using different policies like unfavourable trade relations and economic sanctions. There have been comments by political thinkers that there are covert intentions in foreign policies pursued by Western countries that intervene in the affairs of less powerful countries on the pretext of offering various types of assistance while eyeing the resources of energy and minerals in these latter countries (Andreas Wenger, Robert W. Ofttung and Jerovnim Perovic 2009).

Within nations, economic disparities exist among demarcated groups and within a group among its individual members or families or household units. It is like a jigsaw puzzle, with some being relatively wealthier than others where the demarcations are ambiguous. At the individual level, there are largely two categories: "those who have the means" and "those who do not" for survival and for a "quality of life".

The concept of "*quality of Life*" has been developed to measure the socio-economic situation of groups of people. This term indicates a notion of human welfare or well-being measured by social indicators also, apart from economic indicators of income and expenditure (United Nations). The quality of life includes not only wealth and employment, but also the environment, physical and mental health, education, recreation and leisure time, and also 'social belongingness'. Since 1990, the United Nations Development Programme has quantified "the Human Development Index" (HDI) of countries in terms of such things as education, length of life, availability of clean drinking water, as well as income. India's HDI value, according to UNDP's 2010 Human Development Report, is only 0.519 as against that of the first-ranking Norway, namely, 0.938, but when the HDI is calculated after adjusting for inequality, India's HDI value falls much further to 0.365 which is a loss of 29.6 per cent (UNDP, 2010). This fall in HDI value indicates the exclusion of the underprivileged from the benefits of social and economic development.

Economic and social wealth is the main instrument for indicating status in the jigsaw puzzle of development in its various forms in the world. Currently, being in possession of nuclear power and sophisticated warfare equipments are cited as being indices of the status of wealthy and powerful nations. A nation or an individual can accumulate wealth, but if the wealth is not used strategically in interaction with others or to produce further wealth, then it has no perceived value. Therefore, implied in the term economic wealth is also the term social wealth as economic wealth is put to use for raising the status of the holder.

Therefore, if we examine the jigsaw puzzle a little more closely, we find various combinations of the level of monetary wealth, the level of its utilization to produce goods and services and its interactivity with social wealth, meaning the relative harmony and integration within a nation, a society, a cultural group and, at the grassroots level, a community of families.

In terms of social reality, a simple illustration of a case study given below might serve to illustrate the meaning of different perceptions of poverty. A group of bureaucrats were taken to see bio-technological development in a village such as bio-gas, water-shed development and such like. When they asked to see the living habitats of the "Scheduled Castes", they were shown a poor woman's hamlet on the periphery of the village. She was preparing a meager meal, probably insufficient for her household for the day. In contrast, the group was also shown the sumptuous meal prepared in the *Pradhan*'s house using biogas, whereas the poor woman was using only cow-dung cake. This disparity indicates that development is geared towards the status of the better off and not the less well-off. To the visiting bureaucrats, this incident served to give them a perception of the differences between the poor and the better off not only in terms of economic status but also social status.

The only knowledge that the poor have of aid being given by foreign countries is when these donors visit their project areas to which they have donated money. Then, all that the target group sees is that the *bada saab* has come to see what is happening to us with the monies they have given. This makes the target group feels indebted towards the governance which receives the donor money. This is the major perception of the poor have of the better off when the bureaucrats visit their sites. We have several illustrations of rich nations being charity-oriented towards poorer nations. They offer monetary assistance in the form of aid to the poorer nations, covering up the covert nature of their control over these poorer nations. However, the poor in many countries most of the time hardly receive or are even contacted by aid-giving countries or groups in any tangible shape or form (Hancock, Graham, 1989). Some decades ago, US aid to India was in the form of giving food for the poor Indians under its P.L. 480 programme. That was when in the later 1950s and 1960s India was not self-sufficient in staple foods. Food came in the form of wheat that was surplus in the American market and was disposed as "charity" to poorer nations. Such forms of giving charity indicate *surplus wealth* which is used as baits towards poorer nations. Similar scenarios are observable in other rich countries also who give donations to the poor in India. A rich man gives *daan* during festivals in propitiation of or as thanksgiving to the Godheads. The rich nations give what they do not want, while the poor share with others whatever they have without any sense of condescension.

The UN in its Human Development Reports use measures like income, the physical quality of life and such like comparative measures for assessing the comparative wellbeing of different countries, but these are relative abstract terms. At the ground level of social reality, they cannot measure the extent of anguish and suffering of the poor who are without basic necessities for the household. For a long time, India was under feudal and colonial domination. After it was suddenly propelled into the net of democracy with the declaration of Independence, it was totally unprepared for providing for the wellbeing of the majority and to this day, it has not been able to tackle the various needs of those who were born poor and lacked opportunity to increase their economic status.

The poor in India are unable to make decisions on their own and do not have the power of successful participation in decision-making in development. They have less ability to seek help from the Government and from donor resources. The poor face impediments in accessing economic and social institutions for assistance. The more isolated the groups are from the administrative and organizational hub of the Government, the less access they have to these resources.

There are also dimensions of poverty that relate to structural and transitional poverty variables. These two frames exist especially amongst the poor such as where there is little access to land ownership. This happens because for generations land utilized by the poor was not legally documented, but came down over the years from one generation to another and land was utilized on an informal basis. The poor were mostly agricultural labourers or at the most share-croppers working on the lands of the better off agriculturists. Over-time, many farmers have sold their land to booming industries and, therefore, are in possession of monetory wealth unlike the wealth of property which in their areas did not pay well. Once this poor farmer had money in their hands, they utilized it to move to urban areas and improve their economic status such as becoming builders and contractors, unlike their previous existence where their lands were infertile for agricultural produce.

The poverty status of the majority of the Indian people is also directly related to the implementation of poverty alleviation programmes and subsidies given to the poor. There is lack of proper identification of the really needy among the poor. The developmental agents working in the field are unable, at times, to compute accurate figures and tables. Therefore, it appears that poverty is often inaccurately reported whether by intent or accident (Bonfiglioli, Angelo, 2003).

There are other factors which influence poverty depending upon the interaction of other variables like caste, ethnicity and regionality.

What do we mean exactly when we use the term poverty? Is it only in relation to economic wealth? Or is it combined with social well-being? How much is economic wealth related to social wealth? Does social wealth depend upon economic wealth or is it vice a versa? Or, to put it in another way, does economic wealth produce social wealth? To answer these difficult questions realistically, would mean to interpret the existence of poverty per se. It would mean a specific place, a specific group and a specific time. Economic wealth produces infrastructure facilities, goods and services for the utilisation of those who live within these networks. Among the rich elite, wealth is safeguarded by security guards, safe deposit vaults, investments in the banks which protect the richness of the rich. Others who live at survival levels do not have any security and, therefore, live a day-to-day fragile existence. At the most, a shepherd might communicate that sheep are his wealth while a desert-living person might indicate that camels are his wealth. Thus, living a life of wellbeing implies a well-padded lifestyle for some in contrast to others who are not in comfort as they lack the padding of economic well being. At the same time, economic wealth does not automatically indicate social wellbeing. The saying "uneasy lies the head that wears the crown" in a subtle way implies that the rich have to labour more to preserve their riches. By "social wellbeing" we mean positive social interaction, attitudes and values which are harmonious with others. Certainly not everybody is either rich or poor. There are many "in betweens" Assessing economic wealth is factual. Ascertaining social wealth depends on the interpretation used at a given time in relation to the interaction among people living together. Tribals in India, for instance, as a group are economically poor, but because of the inherent loyalty, sharing and compassion among them, they are socially well off. Wealthy people are more often than not stingy as they like to protect their wealth. Or, to put it euphemistically, they like to garner more wealth. It is often said ironically that the more wealthy a nation or human being is, the greater is the tendency to accumulate more.

In the Indian context, "poverty" is present both in the economic as well as the social contexts. In the economic context, the estimate by the National Sample Survey Organisation of India indicates that the "poor" in 2004-05 were 21.8 per cent of the countrv's population. It was also reported that this came down to 20.4 per cent in 2005-06. The National Sample Survey Organisation (NSSO) of India measured poverty mainly on the basis of the number of food calories consumed, the level of income and the kind of dwelling they lived in. The reduction in poverty was 1.4 percent, which is almost twice the trend observed between 1993-94 and 2004-05. This is mainly because of the growing rate of the GDP in a progressive manner ("India is redefining poverty" at http://www.ifrtd.org accessed on 17. 6. 2011). However, a growing GDP does not imply that the number of the poor has been reduced as the per capita income is highly skewed in favour of the wealthy that make up a minimal number of the population. Therefore, the official statistics on GDP and the reduction in poverty fails to reflect the number of people in India who are not covered by the basic mandates enjoined in the Constitution for bringing about equality.

The Constitution of India in its Preamble has set the goal of achieving equality for all of its citizens. The equality here is defined as both equality of opportunity as well as equality of status. It naturally follows from this that equality also means equal access for all to all the facilities and resources. The poor in India have less of all the above. In the West, homogeneity prevails in terms of dwellings, transport and such like aspects. This is not so in India. The poor can only see cars go by, but do not possess one. Many of them even do not possess a bicycle for transport, whereas in the

West, almost every household has a car, a refrigerator, a washing machine and such like electrical gadgets.

The Indian government has recently decided that India's poor will be defined on the basis of access to six basic amenities, in addition to calories consumed. In this new system, "poverty" is also to be measured with reference to facilities like quality education, access to adequate health facilities, adequate infrastructure, clean and hygienic environment and essential benefits for women and children (Chauhan, Chetan, 2009).

A further problem in assessing poverty in India is that the poor cover a large geographical territory, almost equivalent to being a sub-continent. India has got about 1.2 billion people and 22 recognized official languages besides about 400 other dialects spoken by the people belonging to hundreds of distinct ethnic groups and tribes in a variety of regional and ecological areas. Thus, this heterogeneity makes it more difficult to measure economic wellbeing as there is no one standard that can be homogeneously used.

The Eleventh Five Year Plan had made a resounding rhetoric of reduction in the uneducated and the building up of health infrastructures (Government of India, Planning Commission, December, 2006). Evaluation of this Plan programmes are not adequate and do not give a picture of social reality. This is perhaps because the resources deployed for the field-level evaluation are limited or the evaluators are inadequately trained.

A law has been enacted for the Right to Education of all children, implying that no one child should be debarred from achieving a high quality of education for want of finance. There are some States which offer incentives like free uniforms, free books and mid-day meals. Yet, there are some others which do not give such incentives. Therefore, the very implementation of such programmes is lopsided. There are efforts to expand out-of-school learning to improve the education status of those who previously either did not have access or the opportunity to acquire a fairly satisfactory level of school education. How far it has been successful will only be known by evaluations either mid-term or at the end of the plan period.

Included in the XI Five Year Plan were statements about improved infrastructure, provision of electricity to all households by 2009, economic growth rate, agricultural growth rate and the provision of internet services in villages. These are strategies which are ironical when viewed against the fact that India has about 25 per cent or so below the poverty line, where the individuals are just eking out a minimum level of living. These indicators and targets are sanctimonious statements for which the rhetorical ability of the leaders is famous for.

There continues to be much of little happening, inspite of the rhetoric. Several of the poor, especially in rural and tribal areas, do not see the relationship of rote-learning to their occupational skills or the availability of the job opportunities in their geo-ecological areas.

In general, the Plans from the First Five Year Plan up to the latest Plan have been lacking in appropriate strategies at the ground level to meet the needs of the poor. It is well-known that there is much conniving going on in the allotment of tenders for the construction of infrastructures. These public infrastructures, transport systems, roadway, bridges and other such facilities for the general public are of such poor quality that they succumb quickly due to the poor quality of materials, maintenance and care and siphoning of monies through illicit commissions.

It is significant to note that some Indian states are poorer than even some countries in the sub-Saharan areas of Africa (Sabina Alkire and Maria Santos, July 2010). Such being the situation, we cannot lump all the States in India together as being indexed by homogeneous variables. There is much heterogeneity among groups, whether among States or among smaller groups. Therefore, there needs to be a multi-dimensional interactive set of variables set on similar parameters when comparing one group with another within the country. For example, we cannot compare the sub-culture of one state with another as they are heterogeneously varied. For instance, comparing the sub-culture of Maharashtra with the sub-culture of Bihar will only provide contrasts and not comparability. The above detailed explanation indicates that development is composed of many degrees of varying influences and, therefore, comparisons and contrasts of development should take into account the interaction and degree of these variables in each of the heterogeneous groups. Because of the heterogeneity that defies comparison, there will always be a difference between the conglomerate poverty of one state and another.

There have to be circumstances to allow the situational

determinants to occur similarly. Probably the major situational determinant is the ownership of land. Other situational variables which influence levels of economic status are technology and the extent of industrialisation to which the poor are hardly related.

In 1995, an NGO summit put together quite a few platitudes which seem to have covered almost everything related to wellbeing. Those specified as related to the poor were reduction of poverty, sustained job employment and enhancement of equality (World Summit for Social Development, 1995). In reality, it is well-known that such achievements are difficult to realize.

It is also reported that there is a correlation between the Gross National Product and poverty. However, questions may be asked: Does growth gets shared equally or proportionately or if the GDP goes up for the rich, does some of it trickle down to the poor? Does the GDP contribute to the well-being of all equally? How does it help to the contribution of equality in a nation ridden by discriminations? Does Gross National Product relate mainly to basic essentials, or does it go beyond the latter, and to what extent does it do so? The fact remains that there have been many attempts to find various ways of relating poverty to other variables. Finally, however, in the last analysis, it relates to the totality of wellbeing in several spheres of economic and social equilibrium. We note that poverty is sometimes indexed by several factors together or alone, but mainly by economic lacunae. When giving a generic description of the growth rate, in a given country, it does not usually take into consideration how it affects those who are statistically below the average. While it is known that there are many ranges of poverty, there is absolute poverty which is indexed by hunger and malnutrition. There is relative poverty indicating differences between one group and another in terms of basic necessities, and yet there are other points of perception which relate to richness and comfort which usually is not available to most people in the country. This changing scenario of assessment of poverty is, therefore, a relative perception. However, in developing countries, this is known living below the line of having basic necessities for physical and social well-being that contributes directly to economic poverty (Ravallion, Martin, 2001).

To assess poverty level, two important indices are the Consumer Price Index for Industrial Workers (CPIIW) and the

Consumer Price Index for Agricultural Labourers (CPIAL). Therefore the Consumer Price Index (CPI) is an important measure for assessing standards of living.

Added to the qualification of the dimension of the poor is the "gender factor". It is well-known that female children have relatively less schooling than male children. This is more apparent in poor families where the young, especially the female, are expected to contribute to household chores and occupations. It is possible that female children are sent to schools if there are such incentives as mid-day meal programmes, free text books and uniforms and such like incentives. Otherwise, most poor households find it difficult and unnecessary to send female children to school since they are more needed in the household. The case of female education in Himachal Pradesh is an illustration of this point where there are attractive incentives to send female children to primary schools (Dreze Jean and Kingdom G.G. 2001).

Thus, poverty is not only economic, but is also related to a host of other variables such as education, health, hygiene and dwelling (K. P. Kannan and G. Reveendran, 2011). These variables are weighted differently in different geo-ecological regions dependent upon the productivity of the ecology. For example, in the Thar Desert the standard of hygiene is highly related to sustainable development as there is lack of water to produce food and maintain hygienic conditions. The structural economies of different States in India differ with differential development in infrastructure, industrialisation and human development. In addition, there are some which are governed by political parties which differ from others like, for instance, Trinamool Congress in West Bengal, AIDMK in Tamil Nadu, the Bharatiya Janata Party in Karnataka and Madhya Pradesh, the Samajwadi Party in Uttar Pradesh, the Janata Dal (United) in Bihar besides the Congress at the Centre and in many States, all of whom have somewhat differential policy statements about the priorities of their parties with reference to development. Each of these Parties have their agenda. By and large, the agenda relates to their own aggrandizement, although their own written policies are full of philanthropy and commitment to the cause of the nation.

REFERENCES

"India is redefining poverty" at http://www.ifrtd.org accessed on 17. 6. 2011.

Andreas Wenger, Robert W. Ofttung and Jerovnim Perovic (2009), *Energy and the Transformation of International Relations*, Oxford University Press, USA.

Bonfiglioli, Angelo, 2003, *Empowering the Poor: Local Governance for Poverty Reduction*. New York; United Nations Capital Development Fund.

Chauhan, Chetan, August, 2009, "India Alters Its Definition of Poverty", *The Hindustan Times*, 19 August, 2009.

Dreze Jean and G.G. Kingdom, 2001. "School participation in rural India", *Review of Development Economics*, 5, No. 1:1-33.

Government of India, Planning Commission, December, 2006, *Towards Faster and More Inclusive Growth*.

Govt. of India, *National Family Health Survey-3*.

Govt. of India, *Report of the Expert Group to Advise the Ministry of Rural Development on the methodology.for conducting the Below Poverty Line (BPL) Census for 11th Five Year Plan*, September, 2009.

Hancock, Graham, 1989, *Lords of Poverty: The Power, Prestige, and Corruption of the International Aid Business*. New York: The Atlantic Monthly Press, pp. 234.

India Health News, December 22, 2007. "Malnutrition Among Indian Children Worse than in Sub-Saharan Africa".

K. M. Ashraf, 2000, *Life and Conditions of the People of Hindustan*. Delhi: Gyan Publishing House.

K. P. Kannan and G. Reveendran, 2011, "India's Common People: The Regional Profile", *Economic and Political Weekly*, Vol. XLVI, No. 38.

Mason, John, Adams Bailes, Mary Beda-Andourou, Nancy Copeland, Teresa Curtis, Megan Deitchler, Leigh Foster, Marianna Hensley, Peter Horjus, Christine Johnson, Tina Lloren, Anna Memdez, Mary Munoz, Jonathan Rivers and Gwyneth Vance, 2005, 'Recent Trends in Malnutrition in Developing Regions: Vitamin A Deficiency, Anaemia, Iodine Deficiency, and Child Underweight', *Food and Nutrition Bulletin*, Vol 26, No 1, pp 59-162.

Ravallion, Martin, 2001, "Growth, Inequality and Poverty: Looking Beyond Averages", *World Development*, Elsevier, Vol. 29 (11), pp. 1815.

Sabina Alkire and Maria Santos, 2010, *Multinational Poverty Index, Oxford Poverty and Human Development Initiative*. www.ophi.org.uk)

Saran R. 2003, "How We Live: Census, India Household Survey' *India Today*, 20 July, pp. 343-42)

Sinha, J.B.P., 1977, "The Poverty Syndrome, Power Motive and Democratisation of Work Place", *Integrated Management*, 12 (2), 5-8.

UNDP, 2010. Human Development Report, accessed at http://hdr.undp.org/en/media/HDR_2010_EN_Table 3_reprint.pdf.

World Bank, 2001, *World Development Report: 2000-2001: Attacking Poverty.* New York: Oxford University Press.

World Summit for Social Development, Denmark, 6-12 March, 1995, *Challenges for NGOs.*

2

Demography and the Socio-Economic Variables of Poor Communities

India is a country uniquely different from others, for, unlike others, it has a deeply embedded caste system defining the structure of and relations in the social group. When the people of the same caste or ethnic group live for generations in the same geo-ecological area, they tend to call themselves members of "a community". This sense of community and identity form the most significant aspect of the Indian culture. Though every Indian is said to be possessing a cultural attribute of "Indianness", every Indian also belongs to a specific community which has a specific sub-culture (Jodhka, S., 2001). A community is also seen as an active part of the socio-political scenario. In the Indian case, we might equate the "community" to the term "*Jati*", which in the days of the pre-colonial society was said to identify the members of an occupational group having definite rank and status within the total society. Being a member of a *Jati* or community gives an individual a better picture of his own place in society and his identity. This social identity also offers him security. We often hear the saying that "*woh meri jaat ka hai, mujhe unko madad karna hai*" (He belongs to my caste/community and I have to help him).

The meaning of a community lies in the cohesion of a group in terms of shared social values and attitudes. This cohesion keeps it distinct from other identifiable groups. India as a territorial country has several hundreds of such communities, the larger ones fissioning out into smaller sub-communities. They take their identity as collective and collateral as belonging to a certain spatial area where within that area, occupations tend to be co-relative.

The poor in India largely belong to the lower caste groups. In the overall structure of the Indian caste system of the old, the lower castes offered services to the upper castes who in turn gave them protection and favours (Wiser, William Henricks, 1969). Transferred to the present day context, the same jajmani-type relations exist between politicians in a constituency and its constituent members.

However, the Indian, irrespective of caste or ethnicity, subscribes to a holistic and systematic socio-religious system of norms. Inspite of the secular Constitutional directives, the religious interactions of a caste group empowers plurality so that at one and the same time in the present democratic system the individual subscribes to socio-religious norms while tangentially acknowledging the secular norms. Given the socio-religious norms, the poor from the lower castes subscribe to the principles of the caste system and are thus beholden to the upper castes. Therefore, both from the viewpoint of the religion and from the viewpoint of the socio-economic status, the poor are at the lower rung.

The implications of the constitutional principles of Justice, Equality and Fraternity are relatively unknown terms especially to many Indians of the lower socio-economic groups, who in any case had not been exposed to such principles of political democracy before the break with the colonial period of domination and, what is worse, they have always been illiterate and segregated. Among these three principles of the Constitution, the term equality is a bugbear of most discrepancies in the socio-economic structures and the systems prevalent in the Indian society. Caste is a divisive force, for it operationalises the differences in discriminatory social behaviour.

Both in pre-colonial and colonial periods, the traditional societal values based on the Indian caste system were very strong and determined the social, economic and political life of the masses. The principle of equality was not a virtue espoused in Indian society in those periods, especially in the village communities. Socio-religious discrimination is still prevalent in the traditionally oriented rural areas, which have hardly been touched by secularism, though there have been efforts by many social reformers and intellectuals in the beginning of the nationalist awakenings against the colonial rule to evoke the ideals of social equality.

The terms "Harijan" and "Adivasis" have been replaced by

the Constitutional terms of Scheduled Castes and Scheduled Tribes. So while the connotation remains in an economic form, it is cleared of the old-age attitudes of viewing and treating these social classes as *neech* (lowly) and *achyut* ("Untouchable"). Apparently many of these categories because of the removal of this veil have access to better opportunities if they attempt to do so. Therefore, the poor are mostly those who are economically poor.The post-Independence Indian society became exposed to the principle of equality in the current social change and technological era. This appears to be happening especially in the urban areas. The vulnerability of the poor is co-related with their lessened productive skills and self-esteem in the general society.

At this point we need to explicate clearly who the poor are. The poor make up the vulnerable and fragile population. The poor in societies of the developing world is that proportion who are relatively uneducated and un-skilled.

The demography of India is constantly changing in relation to the increasing and shifting population. Added to this is the heterogeneity in its sub-populations of different castes, creeds, and ethnic groups. The very young in India who are in the age range of the unproductive population (5 to 14 years) are about 251 million. This is the future generation of India. In the current demographic trend of increase in the population, it stands to reason that the increase in the MMR and the IMR are high in the poorer sections which believe in producing large numbers of children. If this situation continues to exist, a larger proportion of Indians would continue to be unproductive and this unproductive range will not diminish in size appreciably. This proportion is probably less in urban areas, than in rural. They are possibly more in the lower castes.

Unfortunately, the young and the unproductive make up demographically the largest proportion of the poor in India. There is a smaller proportion of the productive young who have to care for the larger unproductive segments of society, namely, children, females and the elderly.

As we have said before, since caste is a divisive factor, it is well-known that the upper castes occupy the top professional and business classes. On the other hand, the lowest castes are engaged in menial work, casual and part-time work doing mainly lowly or unskilled jobs. Demographically, the poor segments of society tend to form a larger proportion in most of the states, especially the central states. Rarely do we find a higher proportion of the upper and middle classes in most of the states. This is inevitable, since in any case the largest proportion of the poor are in all states except perhaps in a few states which are likely to be homogeneous like in the north-eastern States and tribals.

It is said that India is an emerging country in the context of others. However, if we examine the growth State by State, we find that some States are very poor, while others are striding at a fast pace into becoming wealthy States. The sectoral and geo-ecological areas of development differ considerably from one State to another. This means that in some States like Rajasthan, Bihar and Madhya Pradesh, the growth of the economy is so slow that it pulls down the higher national growth rate which is really contributed to by the richer States like Punjab, Gujarat, Haryana and Tamil Nadu followed by Himachal Pradesh and Kerala (Gaurav Datt and Martin Ravallion, 2002).

The data from the National Sample Survey Organization's 61st Round Survey Report give information on States which have a large percentage of people living under the poverty line (Table 2.1) and States having a lesser percentage of people living under the poverty line (Table 2.2).

Table 2.1: States which have large proportion of the population living under poverty line (20 – 40+ %)

S. No.	Name of the State	Percentage of people below poverty line
1.	Orissa	(46.4 %)
2.	Bihar	(41.4 %)
3.	Chattisgarh	(40.9 %)
4.	Jharkhand	(40.3 %)
5.	Uttarakhand	(39.6 %)
6.	Madhya Pradesh	(38.3 %)
7.	Maharashtra	(30.7 %)
8.	Rajasthan	(22.1 %)
9.	Uttar Pradesh	(32.8%)

Source: Govt. of India, NSSO, 61st Survey Report

Table 2.2: States which have Less proportion of the population living below the poverty Line

Sl. No.	*Name of the State*	*Percentage of people below poverty line*
1.	Jammu & Kashmir	5.4
2.	Punjab	8.4
3.	Himachal Pradesh	10.0
4.	Haryana	14.0
5.	Delhi	14.7
6.	Kerala	15.0
7.	Andhra Pradesh	15.8
8.	Gujarat	16.8
9.	Assam	19.7

Source: Govt. of India, NSSO, 61st Survey Report (2004-05)

There is a close correlation between high poverty rates and natural population growth rates. Natural population growth rates are higher in the poor States of Bihar (21.5), Rajasthan (20.6), Uttar Pradesh (20.5) Madhya Pradesh (19.2), and Jharkhand (18.6) than the national average (15.2) (Registrar General of India, 2011). There seems to be also a close correlation between poverty and Infant Mortality Rates (IMR) (the number of infant deaths per thousand live-births) which are 67 in Madhya Pradesh, 65 in Orissa, 63 in Uttar Pradesh, 59 in Rajasthan, 54 in Chattisgarh and 52 in Bihar. (*Ibid*)

Further, the poorer States indicated in Table 2.1 above have also large proportions of the population who are illiterate.

Table 2.3: Literacy Rates in Poor States in India

Sl. No.	*Name of the State*	*Literacy Rate*
1.	Bihar	63.8
2.	Jharkhand	67.6
3.	Uttar Pradesh	69.7
4.	Rajasthan	69.7
5.	Andhra Pradesh	67.7
6.	Meghalaya	75.5
7.	Orissa	73.5

Source: Census of India, 2011

The population of the above poor and low literacy States consists of many tribals, Scheduled Castes and also poor Muslims and poor women who make up the fragile population.

Table 2.4: Proportion of Scheduled Castes and Scheduled Tribes in Poor States

Sl. No.*	*Name of States*	*Percentage of Scheduled Castes Population*	*Percentage of Scheduled Tribes Population*
1.	Orissa	16.53	22.19
2.	Bihar	15.72	0.92
3.	Chattisgarh	11.61	31.82
4.	Jharkhand	11.84	26.34
5.	Uttarakhand	17.87	3.02
6.	Madhya Pradesh	15.17	20.26
7.	Maharashtra	10.20	8.87
8.	Rajasthan	17.16	12.57
9.	Uttar Pradesh	21.15	0.07

Sources: Census of India, 2001

The poor States of Bihar, Jharkhand, Madhya Pradesh, Orissa, Rajasthan and Uttar Pradesh contain the 100 districts of India which were ranked the lowest in "Child Development Index" evolved in 2009 by Indicus Analytics for UNICEF (*UNICEF, 2009*). In 2011, an Indian NGO, Naandi Foundation, collected and analysed data from these 100 districts to see the extent of malnutrition prevailing in these districts. Tables 2.5 and 2.6 show the results of data on malnutrition indexed by underweight in these 100 districts:

Table 2.5: Percentage of malnourished children 0-59 months indexed by Underweight, by sex

Malnourishment Indicator	*All Children*	*Boys*	*Girls*
Underweight	42.3	41.0	41.4

Table 2.6: Percentage of malnourished children 0-59 months indexed by Underweight, by mother's education

Education level/Class completed	*Percentage of under-weight children*
None-Can't read	44.7
< 5	40.3
5-7	38.2
8-9	34.5
10+	26.9

The Table 2.6 indicates that where there is poverty and poor educational levels of mothers, there is a high incidence of malnourishment among children.

Therefore, in examining the dissimilarities existing between the poor and the rich in these States, we see that influential extraneous variables also increase the dissimilarity. These variables are the increased number of malnourished children, illiteracy, especially among mothers, and Infant Mortality. These three variables interact to give the poor a low profile in terms of well-being. Overarching these variables is the powerful variable of caste. We saw from Table 2.4 above that Scheduled Castes and Scheduled Tribes exist in large numbers in these poorer States, adding to the fragility of the poor.

Another depressing variable in the poverty status of the majority population of India is that as in the days of the old, the country is ruled by the nexus of the politician, the bureaucrat and the corporate world. Peter A. Gourevitch & James Shinn, 2007), using evidence from 39 countries of Europe, Asia and Africa, state that the power of the corporate organisations is shaped by political governance. This may also apply to India.

We give in the Table 2.7 below a concise summary of the analysis of the States in relation to the percentage of the poor, domestic product, per capita income, and monthly per capita expenditure.

While the total number of poor in India is 27.5 per cent or over a quarter of the total population, there are differences from State to State. Orissa has the greatest proportion of the poor among all the States with 46.4 per cent, followed by Bihar (41.4%), Chhattisgarh (40.9%), Jharkhand (40.3%), Madhya Pradesh (38.3%), Uttar Pradesh (32.8%), Maharashtra (32.2%) in that order. These are States where about one-third or more of the population are categorized as poor. The States which have less than 20 per cent of their population as poor are Punjab (8.4%), Haryana (14%), Kerala (15%), Delhi (15.2%), Gujarat (16%), and Assam (19.75%).

It is said, however, that there is a tendency for the top levels of these lower castes to try and imitate the behaviour of the upper castes. This phenomenon is a kind of reassembling of concepts which describes Srinivas's Sanskritisation and Westernisation themes, where whenever possible the lower classes attempt to imitate the behaviour of the upper. However, given the fact that

Table 2.7: Summary of States in relation to the Percentage of the Poor, Domestic Product, Per Capita Income, and Monthly Per Capita Expenditure

Sl. No.	*Name of the States*	*Population proportion*	*Net State Domestic Product (NSDP) (2009-10) (in Rs. crore)*	*Per capita income (2009-10) (Rs per annum)**	*Contribution to Central Income Tax (2007-08)*	*Percentage of the poor*	*Monthly Per Capita Consumer Expenditure*
1.	Maharashtra	9.28 (2)	817,891	74027 (2)	37.09 (1)	32.2 (8)	1795
2.	Uttar Pradesh	16.49 (1)	453,020	23132 (17)	7.49 (2)	32.8 (7)	1237
3.	Andhra Pradesh	7.00	426,816	51025 (7)	3.92 (6)	27.5 (9)	1736
4.	Tamil Nadu	5.96	417,716	62499 (4)	6.42 (4)	22.5 (12)	1554
5.	Gujarat	5	370,400	63961 (3)	3.90 (7)	16.8 (15)	1509
6.	West Bengal	7.55 (3)	366,318	41469 (10)	4.48 (5)	24.7 (11)	1459
7.	Karnataka	5.05	296,720	50,676 (8)	7.35 (3)	25.0 (10)	1537
8.	Rajasthan	5.67	226,710	34,189 (12)	1.44 (11)	22.1 (13)	1421
9.	Delhi	1.38	207,180	116,886	16.01 (2)	15.2 (16)	—
10.	Kerala	2.76	202,487	59,179	0.91	15.0 (17)	2124
11.	Haryana	2.09	195,762	78,781	1.71	14.0 (18)	1916
12.	Madhya Pradesh	6.00	192,333	27,250	1.81 (along with Chattisgarh)	38.3 (6)	1285
13.	Punjab	2.30	177,179	62,153	0.85	8.4 (21)	1879
14.	Bihar	8.58	154,503	16,119	0.92 (including Jharkhand)	41.4 (2)	1009
15.	Orissa	3.47	134,242	33,226	1.44	46.4 (1)	1183
16.	Jharkhand	2.72	94,814	30,719	0.92 (along with Bihar)	40.3(4)	1205
17.	Chhattisgarh	2.11	93,245	38,059	1.81 (along with MP)	40.9 (3)	1216
18.	Assam	2.58	81,691	—	0.66	19.7 (14)	1379
19.	Uttarakhand	0.84	54,435	55,877	7.49 (along with UP)	39.6 (5)	—
20.	Himachal Pradesh	0.57	35,593	50,365	< 0.90	10.0 (20)	—
21.	Goa	0.12	22,283	132,719	0.72	13.8 (19)	—
	India	100	52,98,129	52,98,129	100	27.5	1519

*RBI Handbook of Statistics on Indian Economy 2010-11.

there is the reservation policy for education and for jobs, for these poor who also belong to the schedule castes and schedule tribes, there is still much to be desired in terms of availability of opportunities for them, especially since they are marginalized, and since they have to spend much of their work-a-day world in earning a livelihood to survive.

Another phenomenon that accrues to the poor is that while they are forgotten during most of the time, when it comes to elections they are the most sought after as they can be bought up by an ironic system called cash for votes. These poor are committed to those politicians in their constituencies for whom they vote at election times, which then gives these politicians a large clout to manipulate those who voted for them and great dependency of these voters on the politicians whom they voted for. This seems like a revival of the jajmani system. The politicians offer protection and privileges. The voters in turn offer free services hoping to gain favours in their times of need. The lack of experience in educated politics among the poor gives rise to corrupt practices among the politicians (Chaudhury, P., 2007). When the members of the polity are given powerful positions, they tend to favour their own community and kin which, therefore, gives rise to unethical practices like nepotism. On the other hand, there are many in the general society who are also corrupt but to avoid punishment act as "whistle blowers" and, therefore, buy their freedom by indicating the real culprits at the top, as is evident, in the case of some recent unsolved scams. However, such "whistle-blowers" are in danger of being eliminated as observed in some of the unresolved cases of so-called suicides and murders of such people who are close to the corrupt polity.

In governance, the caste system occupies an important role, differentiating the population into those who have power and the means and those who do not have. Further, castes differentiate between those who are more powerful and those who are powerless. Again, caste also differentiates among these groups on a discriminatory basis into socially adhering and socially avoiding groups. The larger proportion of the Indian population belonged to the "lower" castes. Finally, there seems to be a close correlation between the underprivileged, the vulnerable, the lower castes and the less better off, mainly living in the poorer sections of the population.

Caste also assumes political overtones. This was recognized in Marriot's writing about "great" and "little" traditions described as the higher and lower castes (Marriot, M., 1955) and explained in Milton Singer's book Structure and Change in Indian society. (Singer, Milton, 1955-56). This network spread across village societies. It was essential to marry out of one's lineage (*gotra* exogamy), but within the same caste (endogamy). This kept the caste parameters intact. When these lines were crossed, it led to violation of the status of the family, kinship and caste which often led to violence. We see this today in honour killings in North India where crossing gotra barriers lead to violence because of the "dishonor" in marrying out of caste into a lower caste or into the same gotra. Overtime, with the influence of modernisation, globalization and world interactions, these caste differences have become somewhat muted in the work-a-day world of technology and industrialisation. Nevertheless, if a Brahmin knew that a certain person belonged to the Scheduled Castes, he would not interact with him closely for fear of being seen as polluted in the eyes of the public and ostracized. Therefore, there are strict injunctions on the rites of purity and pollution among castes. Since Indians are mainly Hindus living according to the dictates of socio-religious norms, this attitude towards avoidance and "approach" is still followed to this day, especially in traditional, remote rural areas. In far away habitats where groups are usually uneducated, these practices continue in a rigid manner. If pollution occurs, purification rites are performed. Thus, this stronghold of religious beliefs in the caste system is the backbone that guides the values, attitudes and behaviour of Hindus who form the largest proportion of poor Indians. These values and attitudes exist to this day even amongst those who are educated in the secular system of equality and fraternity within the injunctions of the Constitution. Therefore, the values of secularism are often in confrontation with the values of socio-religious beliefs of the society. The latter is often used to the advantage of the upper castes in the political system of governance. Ironically public places are frequented by all castes, who rub shoulders with each other and where it is difficult to distinguish one caste from the other, whether it is in the market or cinema halls or at public events. So the majority of Indians, mainly Hindus, live on a dual track, of secularism, in public places, and traditional religious practices in private household lives. The world of the Indian is still bound to a transient world of reincarnation. The Indian lives in the present world building up on good deeds (karma) to better his life for the next reincarnation. This pattern is more apparent in family, kinship, genealogical and hierarchical affiliations.

In many covert ways the upper castes hold the lower castes under its power using religious symbolism. Consequently, the many religious practices of the upper castes are barriered to the lower castes which in a sense deplete the self-esteem and psychologically prevent them from attaining such privileges mainly available to the upper castes.

Geo-ecologically Indians come from different race groups. The 6 main racial groups are: Negrito; Proto-Australoids or Austrics; Mongoloids; Dravidian; Western Brachycephals; and Nordic Aryans. Ethnicity is a special attribute which can be traced racially, giving these ethnic groups typical physiognomies. They settled down in roughly four territories added on by migrants across land and sea. These four categories relate roughly to those who came from Persia and settled down as Kashmiris and Punjabis. The people who came probably by Sea settled in the Southern Part of India as Dravidians. The people who came down from Mongolia, China and the Far East settled down in the northeastern States. The people on the West Coast are a mixture of the sea-traders who came from partly Persia, and partly from Africa. The different racial groups confined themselves to specific territories in India which allows them the scope of dynamics to interact politically with the other ethnic groups in the country. It is not unusual, therefore, to find that a President can come from south India; a Prime Minister from North India and with several races represented in the bureaucracy at different levels of seniority. It is often said euphemistically that those from the West are usually management and business-oriented, that those from the north are territorial-minded, those from the east the artistic-minded and those from the south are usually known as intellectuals.

Over the ages, these racial-cum-ethnic characteristics were further tied to caste by occupations thus creating caste barriers.

Considering the fact that in the early years India was invaded from all sides, the people who accumulated in Central India were a mix of various ethnic lineages. They took on names similar to those mainly of the north, so that one could find a Singh in Uttar

Pradesh, in Rajasthan, in Bihar, and in Madhya Pradesh (States clustered in Central India). These centralized States were the least touched by developmental programmes and contained a majority of nomads, Dalits and *Adivasis* who were also mainly the poor and continue to be so to this day. There seems that these central states were relatively least touched by developmental services and facilities as compared to the others. The poor in these states remained in the interior areas living on lands of low fertility or in forests that were mainly occupied by tribals.

Arising out of these combinations of varying castes, sub-castes, varying ethnic groups and their varying residential habitats across India, a closer analysis reveals that the more interior a village or a tribal hamlet, the more they are away from the parameters of interaction with other events around them. Therefore, these areas tend to be less developed. We find that there are larger states like Bihar and Madhya Pradesh where interaction is less among villagers since they are scattered from each other, that tradition is closely adhered to, as there are fewer interventions of development in them. For example, a farmer in Madhya Pradesh, even though he has a health centre close to his village, may not utilize it as he is deeply ingrained in the traditional system of health cure by *"jadee bootee"* and the incantations of the *"Jharra"* (medicine men, considered to be holy who could drive away evil spirits), because of deeply ingrained traditional beliefs. Therefore, when well-meaning NGOs and Governmental representatives come around and try to convince the parents of the poor that the children should go to school, and pregnant mothers should attend a healthcare centre, it does not make sense to the household as they are more attached to their traditional ways of medication and informal teachings. This, of course, may be an extreme example, but it serves to illustrate the point that in the villages, the lower castes who also tend to be poor, are generally out of touch with the developmental programmes. These poorest segments are the very fragile people of India who are most affected by political maneuverings which are the usual strategies used by the upper castes, who also tend to be the politicians, leaders and better offs.

After Independence and with the introduction of compilation of social, economic, educational, demographic and other data during the Decennial census operations, much is now known about household-level details. The National Sample Survey Organisation

(NSSO) also brings out periodic reports which indicate that the social categories of Scheduled Tribes and Scheduled Castes are the most underprivileged. They are socially, educationally and economically deprived. There is high inequality in assets. The top 5 per cent of Indians possess 38 per cent of the total assets and the bottom 60 per cent own a mere 13 per cent. There is one-third high incidence of poverty among Scheduled Castes and Scheduled Tribes and one-third of Muslims live below the poverty line (Rajindar Sachar, 2010).

In view of these facts, although reservation has been granted in education and job opportunities for these marginalized groups, economic deprivation is systemic in their lives.

In a recent "India Human Development Survey" (IHDS) undertaken by the National Council of Applied Economic Research (NCAER) and the University of Maryland, a study was conducted on a sample of 41,554 households. The analysis of the data from this survey has revealed that the socio-economic attributes of the low socio-economic categories tend to exclude them from the mainstream of society, thus ratifying the fact that those who tend to be lower in these attributes are indifferently treated in the developmental schema of governance (Sonalde B. Desai, Amaresh Dubey, Brij Lal Joshi, Mitali Sen, Abusaleh Shariff, and Reeve Vanneman, 2010). Along with Scheduled castes and scheduled tribes, a majority of poor Muslim communities and women form the most disadvantaged groups (Govt. of India, 2006). Among these disadvantaged sections, women are the most underprivileged. The largest occupational group among the chronically poor is casual agricultural labourers (Aastha Kapur Mehta, Shepherd, 2006).

When we talk about development in terms of GDP growth rate, a factor that gets obscured is related to the number of new jobs created. Previous to 2004, when the National Democratic Alliance was in power, 62 million jobs were created. However this number has fallen down drastically to 2 million during the first term of governance (2004-2009) by the current governing coalition of parties (UPA) even though India's Planning Commission has targeted for 58 million jobs for the five years from 2007 to 2012. The situation still remains dismal. The fall in job creation took place even while the GDP grew by about 8.43 per cent annually. This disjuncture indicates that the increase in GDP is not the product of increased jobs for the people but it is because of the fact that technology has taken over and displaced man-power for the production of wealth. Though India is said to have withstood the global recession of 2008, its GDP growth rate has been fluctuating and has fallen from about 9 percent in the year 2009 to about 6.5 per cent in 2012. This has further weakened the capacity of market forces to create new job opportunities in the organised sectors. A Government of India survey in 2010 has revealed that only 59 out of 1000 persons are in the wage/salaried employment (Government of India, 2010).

The people who are in the agricultural sector and in the informal urban labour sector are the ones that suffer the most, especially exacerbated due to the rising consumer price index.

If the argument is taken further, the low educational status of the poor is related to lowered health, greater morbidity, less productive days of work and, therefore, a drop in the earning capacity of a household at the marginal level. As we have said before, this is probably due to the world-wide recession but more importantly due to the fact that the ruling party in India which has made promises for sustainable development has not been able to fulfil its promises. Further, the situation is worsened because the poor for the slight crimes are penalized and are unable to free themselves since they do not understand the law, nor their rights, and they cannot afford lawyers to fight their cases. On the other hand, we have observed that a Minister jailed for corruption can employ expensive lawyers and thus easily get bail. We have also witnessed incredible scenes where a jailed Minister went out on bail and had second thoughts on realizing that it did not suit his political profile. He then returned to jail for the treatment inside the jail. Such like curious strategies are being wielded about in order to hoodwink justice and stay outside the jail on bail as long as possible or delay their cases till they attrition out of sight of the public and, therefore, appeals will continue. For instance, the case of a Minister who was reported to have been involved in the Commonwealth Games scam existed in high profile for a day or two and then fell out of sight. Similarly, such suspect cases have been discovered in many States. They are alive for a certain time and then fall back into obscurity. These corrupt senior members are high profiled in their activities, spurred on by the opposition. Such scams are coming to the surface in such quick fashion that one does not know from day to day as to what the next scam would be and many of them are related to seasoned senior politicians.

If the lowest communities are at the lowest rung of development in the Indian scenario, what are the chances that they would be able to attain a better status in the years to come? This is yet unknown. However, we might offer some "guestimates" about the dynamics of the lower classes. The efforts of the governance, however, are not in consonance with the efforts of the people themselves, especially the middle classes, who are, so to speak, "raising themselves up by their own bootstraps". One such example is the attempt of the poor to raise their status by rushing to urban areas for better job opportunities. A tribal who goes to the metropolis for earning a better income since his land has been probably usurped or recompensed for a paltry sum by industrial corporations, often tends to have a dual social network, one in his place of origin and another in his place of work in the urban area. Therefore, such people not only suffer from deprivation but also are dividing their identity between these two locales.

The survey of the NCAER stated above reveals that the better-off States have better facilities than the poor States, which therefore offer better facilities for raising one's status in the better-off States. However, these so-called better opportunities are merely myths as the rural migrant in an urban slum has less of a social profile than which existed in his original rural surroundings. On all these counts, therefore, the poor States where there are large numbers of excluded and disadvantaged people are: Orissa, Bihar, Chattisgarh, Jharkhand, Rajasthan, Uttar Pradesh, Madhya Pradesh and West Bengal. Besides lesser availability of the major developmental facilities, what other factors make for the difference between the rich and poor States? By and large, there is lack of political will to institute such facilities for the marginalized in the poorer States, given the fact that taken together the poor in these poor States form the largest proportion of voters who are exploited by politicians at the time of elections and hold these voters under their control. There exists lack of efforts by politicians to ensure that benefits of developmental programmes reach the poor in these States. Several scams that have come to the limelight in 2010 and 2011 lend truth to this assessment. The smaller proportion of the better off in these states are knowledgeable enough to know that if the poor have widened awareness, knowledge and facilities, they might not vote for them during elections and, further still, might assert their own free will without being smothered by the tri-nexus of the politician, the bureaucrat and the corporate world. It is well-known that the corporate world is the hidden bank for lobbying for itself with the politician and the administration so as to help them obtain registrations and licenses. They are also known as task masters in the field of "lobbyism".

If we look at the larger map of India, the rich tend to live in urban metropolitan areas, closer to the areas of governance and parliamentary power. The rich during the time of elections come to the forefront with much lobbying in financing favored politicians in order that when the latter is elected the favours of these elected politicians are more easily obtainable. The end result is that both the politician and the corporate man find ways and means to become wealthier and more powerful and thereby more corrupt. The only difference is that the corporate man creates economically favourable situations for the politician to advance policies that meet the corporate needs. Thus, we have an important operative triad, namely, that of the corporate world, the politician, and the bureaucratic executive, who together interact to advance their own needs. Consequently, there must be a larger proportion of the less wealthy, the less politically powerful and those lower in the bureaucratic structure, for the triad nexus to rule over them.

Therefore, it is to the profit of the better off politicians, the powerful people in the corporate world and bureaucrats, to keep the marginalized within marginalized parameters. The latter are always willing to follow the instructions of the Commission agents who represent the triad nexus. In other words, it stands to reason that if these marginalized groups continue to be marginalized, by political maneuvers, then the political favourites who are the better off in these States stand a greater chance of being re-elected and, therefore, being able to continue their machinations over the marginalized in their constituencies. These politicians are also artful who know how and when to throw around little monies to the marginalized in order to gain political power, especially during election times.

After elections, the situation returns to square one and the game continues. Thus, the deep-rooted attitudes remain the same. This affects the notion of equality. To put it bluntly, the servants will still continue to behave like servants and their masters will still continue to behave as masters. No matter, what the title might be, the ruling cap might change from one head to another, but the attitudes and actions of the collective politicians will remain the same whether the cap goes to party "A" or party "B".

The old form of feudalism has a new face. The leaders are no longer Rajas, Nawabs or Zamindars. They are now the political players who are in a sense the overlords of poverty in India. In his book, "Lords of Poverty", Hancock has stated this about the international aid-givers which might as well be attributed to aid for the poor in India. Hancock states about international aid that only a very small portion of the international aid from the developed countries is translated into direct assistance to the needy, *"thanks to bureaucratic inefficiency, misguided policies, large executive salaries, political corruption, and the self-perpetuating 'overhead' of the administrative agencies, much of this tremendous wealth is frittered away"* (Hancock, Graham, 1989, pp. 234).

We still have not found a well-documented answer as to which sections of society have benefited from globalization. If the world market crashes, it affects those in India who sell their products to the west and those who have been rich investors overnight can become paupers because of the fluctuations of the world market and the effect of global recession. Again, overnight a family that has a tradition of living of industries for a long period of time like oil and cotton are now better off in the emerging dynamic changes in the global market because of world trade and commerce encouraging their exports. This is evident in the *nouveau riche* Vaishya caste families who while still carrying on their old traditional habits now have a wider market to invest their profits. The *nouveau riche* who have profited over the years in expanding their small-scale industries like steel, car parts, motor cycles and related equipments have now built their own empires. Some of these extremely rich can buy their own yachts, their own sleek aeroplanes and even may have wedding celebrations in the aeroplanes in the air. Their monetary caches are so monumental that it has led to the current extreme agitation by the growing middle class who are now aware of such hordes of black wealth stashed away. If such wealth is recovered there would probably be no pleading hands asking for *roti, kapda aur makaan*, nor the need for asking for better infrastructure, clean water, and communication facilities for a long time.

The rich, however, tend to retain their socio-cultural values and their socio-religious practices as security blankets even though their monetary wealth is incalculable. So, also, they, like the rural migrants, live in two worlds: the world of commerce and marketing outside their homes and the preservation of the world of caste, family and kinship in their households.

The problem in India is that economic wealth for ages has been the fortress of the feudal kings and lords (zamindars) in the ancient days, the colonialists in the British days, and is now in the hands of those who are politically high up and have easy access to unaccounted wealth. The public accounts system has yet to resolve the issue of unaccounted wealth as there are many unknown hands in the "pot of gold". The Government seems to be making an effort to stem corruption by using the processing of the Lokpal Bill. But, its acceptance or rejection across the spectrum of different political parties is still unknown. In any case, its many convoluted statements do not make sense to the poor as to their application to their daily life. We do not know for whom, when and why these dramas take place. Some underlings have been uncovered but many are hidden behind the obscurant curtain.

These illustrations indicate that those who are powerful and have access to monetary gains will do their best to stamp out any effort which will confront them with their own corruption.

Further, no longer is caste tied to just one occupation as in the days of the old. For instance, an OBC community member through sheer enterprise might climb up the social ladder of power just as quickly as a Kshatriya might. To distinguish between the two in class occupations on the basis of caste is difficult. So we see caste and class existing side by side where they are intertwined in occupational activities but not in the practice of socio-religious interactions. Again, the unskilled are the majority belonging to the lower castes who also have a poor social status. In other countries, social class is an interactive variable of occupation, social standing and education. One might change one's class, but not one's caste or tribe.

Since there is an inter-mix of these variables in the growing environment of high-speed technology, global exchanges and trade and commerce, fluctuating amongst nations, it is likely that the phenomenon of caste will eventually be muted in the generations to come. Right now it is in a period of transition. Caste is still related to social status and to maintain a status quo, it is now being used indiscriminately to control the poor and to pressurize them in their excluded groups.

It seems essential that the politician who stands for election either has wealth or is given wealth by business lobbyists to buy their vote banks. Although the legal prescribed limits of expenditure for electioneering are known, the use of black money is much over and above that amount.

In the previous section, we have attempted to delineate the characteristics of economic deprivation which distinguishes the poor from the rich. Yet, at the same time, the large majority of the poor are powerless even though some of them are gradually entering into the portals of the lower middle class.

It is but natural to expect that individuals who belong to the same community, caste, class, occupation and ethnic group are likely to live in the same residential area. In these formations, the poor tend to cluster with the poor and the rich with the rich, with the poorer clusters being overwhelmingly large, with comparatively little resources.

S. Jodhka raised the questions of culture, community and identities and their place in building a democratic national society (Jodhka, S., 2001). Communities often come together in action to pursue the common goals such as to protest against ecological degradation, as in the case of the participation of tribal peoples and small farmers in the *Narmada Bachao Andolan*. An individual, therefore, has his community identity only when he proclaims that he is part of it and adheres to its norms. The community is not to be taken as a synonym for communism. Communism is an ideology. It stands apart for itself just as the ideologies of autocracy and democracy do for themselves.

REFERENCES

Aastha Kapur Mehta, Shepherd, 2006, *Chronic Poverty and Development Policy*. Delhi: Sage Publications Pvt. Ltd.

Chaudhury, P., 2007, "Caste Politics Keeps India's Poor Divided". The Japan Times, June 24, 2007.

Gaurav Datt and Martin Ravallion, 2002, "Is India's Economic Growth Leaving the Poor Behind?", *Journal of Economic Perspectives*, American Economic Association, Vol. 16 (3), pp. 89-108).

Govt. of India, 2006, *Social and Economic and Educational Status of Muslim Community of India*. A Report by the Prime Minister's High Level (Justice Sachar) Committee.

Government of India, 2010, Report on Employment & Unemployment Survey, 2009-10, Government of India, Ministry of Employment, Labour Bureau, Chandigarh, 2010.

Hancock, Graham, 1989, Lords of Poverty: The Power, Prestige, and Corruption of the International Aid Business. New York: The Atlantic Monthly Press, pp. 234.

Jodhka, S., 2001, *Community and Identities: Contemporary Discourses on Culture and Politics in India*. New Delhi: Sage Publications.

Marriot, M., 1955, Little community in Indigenous Civilization, in N. Marriot (ed.), Village India Studies on Little Communities. Illinois: Chicago University Press.

Peter A. Gourevitch & James Shinn, 2007, Political Power and Corporate Control: The New Global Politics of Corporate Governance, Princeton University Press).

Rajindar Sachar, 2010, "Whither Indian Politics / Elections?", Mainstream, March 2-8, Vol L, No. 11, p. 4.

Registrar General of India, 2011, *SRS Bulletin*, Volume 45, No. 1, January, 2011.

Report on Employment & Unemployment Survey, 2009-10, Government of India, Ministry of Labour & Employment, Labour Bureau, Chandigarh, 2010.

Singer, Milton, 1955-56, 'Cultural Pattern of Indian Civilization: a Preliminary Report of Methodological Field Study', *Far Eastern quarterly*. No. 15, pp. 230-327.

Sonalde B. Desai, Amaresh Dubey, Brij Lal Joshi, Mitali Sen, Abusaleh Shariff, and Reeve Vanneman, 2010, *Human Development in India: Challenges for a Society in Transition*. New Delhi: Oxford University Press. pp. 171-193.

UNICEF, 2009, *The State of the World; Children*.

Wiser, William Henricks, 1969, *The Hindu Jajman System: A Socio-economic system interrelating of members of Hindu community in Services*, Lucknow: Lucknow Publishing House.

3

Power: Its Influence, Homogeneity and Heterogeneity

There is a great deal of interaction between traditionality and modernity affecting power and powerlessness. It is said that India is a land of rich cultural heritage. This heritage has been contributed to by various civilizations. The feudal regimes that existed in India in the past had entrenched the parameters of traditionalism so as to keep the power of the feudal kings and lords intact over the large masses of people.

The British were not interested in altering the socio-cultural system in India. Even though a miniscule proportion of the traditionally rich in India took to western education, they and a large majority of other Indians clung to their traditionalism as the major part of their identity and security. The fulcrum of this traditionalism is the Hindu social system, including its religious and caste system. The caste-cum-traditional occupation status of social groups came to define power relations among the groups in the society in the spheres of social interactions, economy and polity.The maintenance of the tradition implied the maintenance of one's identity in the socio-religious structure of the society. Caste still holds its sway over the masses. Through the principles adopted in its Constitution, independent India subscribed to the ideal of a pluralistic society where people lived harmoniously on an equality basis. This meant that the "lower" castes were not to be denigrated any more in any sphere of social life. However, the discrimination against the "lower" castes arising from traditionalism that India carried with it from its feudal days could not be erased and, therefore, there was a curious confrontation between the values of the caste-based traditional social system and the equality principle of democracy. The entrenched interests in maintaining the traditionality of the caste system was and is still resistant to change. For this reason, the Constitution of India in its various Articles provided for certain special measures for the welfare and development of the traditionally disadvantaged social groups, namely, the Scheduled Castes (SCs), the Scheduled Tribes (STs) and Other Backward Classes. There were also certain other programmes of the Government specifically aimed at improving the socio-economic conditions of these traditionally disadvantaged groups such as pre-matric and post-matric scholarships given to Scheduled Caste and Scheduled Tribe students. There are now increase in educated people among these lower socio-economic groups some of whom have been able to raise their social status and power by gaining dignified employment, mostly in Governmental sectors. That there is opposition to the provision of reservations to SCs and STs from the upper caste sections is mainly a reflection of resistance to the loss of power that was enjoyed exclusively by the upper caste sections. There seems to be an inner struggle between the upper castes and the lower castes in the holding of positions in bureaucracy and in the political arena.

We must also admit that the effect of rapid technological and social changes influence the caste system. The emergence of institutions based on new principles and ideologies, including democracy, equality, and the idea of human dignity and self-respect, have been able, to some extent, to negate the core ideas of the caste system which discriminated between social groups as "upper" and 'lower'. The most telling and tangible evidence of this is the entry of a small section of people from the "lower" social groups into the areas of trade, commerce and industry. A small section belonging to the erstwhile "untouchable" communities have recently formed the Dalit Chamber of Commerce and Industry (DICCI).

The power gained by the erstwhile "untouchable" castes in the area of political representation is the most significant phenomenon. This is more exemplararily observable in Uttar Pradesh, which has a large number of the erstwhile "untouchable" castes, who through their sheer voting power have been able to propel a Dalit woman to the Chief Ministership. It is essential for these poor lower castes to be represented in the political leadership if India is to achieve its Constitutional goal of assuring all of its citizen's equality and liberty.

The realization of the lofty principles of the Indian Constitution, however, is not without barriers and obstacles. There is still much control by the upper castes and upper socio-economic classes of the governance and, therefore, suppression of the needs and priorities of the poor lower castes through covert means. In the face of growing modernisation of production technologies and institutions, the caste distinctions seem to have worn-out and do not appear to have much hold in the public interactions, at least among the urban educated sections. Thus, there is a curious mix of the power of the upper castes and attempts by the lower castes to break these caste barriers. These caste distinctions still work subtly and discretely, and there is still the remnant of the *Jajmani* system which adds to the discriminations almost under cover. As revealed by a study by ICSSR in 42 panchayats across 12 States, headed both by male and female Pradhans, the female representatives and Pradhans and those from the lower castes were excluded from integration with the male upper caste Pradhans and Panchyat Members. Therefore, caste and gender exclusion still continues to play a strong role in the polity and communities (Mathew, George & Baburao Shravan Bhaviskar, 2009).

Given the fact that modernity implies change and traditionality implies preserving status-quo, the two are in constant contradiction with each other. In the face of the unknown future that modernity could bring, for example, sophisticated technology, its good and its debilitating aspects, preservation of identity through holding on to tradition seems to be the foundation for the existence of identity and security. During this transition from traditionality to modernity, there is bound to be some confusion and complexity till the situation rearranges itself (Norbu, Dawa, 1996). Modernity might take hold of the situation in view of the social and technological changes. Still the Indian like the Japanese and the Chinese in their growing economic and power situations will continue to hold on to both sides of the coin, namely, traditionality and modernity. This in a sense gives an upper hand to the upper castes vis-à-vis the lower castes in their race towards holding power.

In India we have a large proportion of farmers who till the land, which is not very fertile, still using elementary methods of cultivation. On the other hand, there are a very miniscule number of landowners who possess sophisticated machinery to produce high quality yields without much physical effort. The latter, therefore, have greater power over the poorer farmers. In the industrial sector, the owner of large industries has a great amount of power over smaller ones.

The agricultural sector has less monetary wealth than the industrial sector. Therefore, by inference, the industrialist has greater power than the agriculturist. Industrialisation which is fast developing in India provides technology which creates better statuses more quickly than does agricultural production. Put together, we can re-categorize the agriculture and the industrial groups into the producer of essential goods like food and the producer of sophisticated goods through technology respectively. The fact remains that the industrialists have a greater hold over the economy than does the agriculturists. In India, there is a greater need for the production of agricultural goods and services as a first step towards wellbeing, especially for the poor who live in large numbers in rural areas. As we have indicated, agriculture production does not fully service the poor. There are instances where the produce is sold abroad by the rich farmers to make themselves richer and more powerful, and thereby depleting the availability of food for the vast masses in rural areas who do not have land for cultivation or exist on non-fertile land (Bhalla, G. S., 1994, Sukhatme, 1965). After the introduction of the LPG (Liberalisation, Privatization and Globalization), the priorities in food production have changed and there are world factors influencing food production. For example, farmers are increasingly shifting to cash crops and, also, large quantities of produce are directed towards agro-industries. Economic commentators have alleged that this shift is partly due to the omission on the part of the Indian planners in protecting livelihood in agriculture, cultivation and in the use of forest produce. It is also alleged that the beneficiaries of infrastructure development which is taking place in India are more likely to be industrialists and land-developers than the agriculturists (Goswami, Rahu, 2011).

We will now discuss the various factors that affect and effect power. In the initial years of the 21st century, there are rapid changes occurring in the economic contexts of the various nations. With the increase in social media and information dissemination technologies, people are becoming more informed about their economic statuses in relation to others. The products of technology accrue mostly to the rich, thereby, widening the gap between the rich and the poor. The riches of the rich are manipulatively used at the time of elections to buy votes in a surreptitious manner and, therefore, represent a source of untold power. In the global arena, different countries of the world have formed "hubs' of international alliances. The western alliances have brought about organisations like the EU, while the UN is an umbrella organisation of both the western and eastern countries. SAARC is an organisation of the South Asian countries. These various international organisations interact with each other but mainly in the area of commerce and trade and in giving and accepting aid. The current economic recession has, however, created imbalances within the Western countries, where the countries which rapidly accumulated sovereign debts like Spain and Greece had to be bailed out. The world is also divided into what is called the North and the South. By and large it is the northern alliances that give aid as donor countries to the poor countries in the south. Perhaps, the power of the Western alliances over the Middle East countries have led them to create inroads into these Middle East countries, some of which have been totally destabilized. For instances, Iraq and Libya. In Iraq, the Government supported by the West after the overthrow of Saddam Hussein is hardly able to contain the sectarian fire of militancy which is still alive and lingering. Egypt after the fall of the autocratic rule of Hosni Mubarak is still to find a way for ushering in liberal democracy. In Syria, the autocratic ruler is facing challenges from a large section of its people who demand liberty. There seems to be a covert manipulation of the eastern countries by the western powers so as to continue to keep the former under the sway of the latter. Many assisted poor countries find themselves in the peculiar situation of being indebted to the Anglo-Saxon countries, although it is said that countries like China and India are emerging as new economic power houses with stability in the economic growth, which is unlike the economic destabilization of some of the countries of the west.

In India, over the recent decades, it is the middle class that is growing steadily in numbers and in economic status. Therefore, the dynamic changes that are occurring are mostly at the top level of the socio-economic classes. The poor steadily continue to be poor and, unfortunately, according to the World Work's Report of 2008, the actual number of poor in India has gone up over the years if it is calculated by taking a daily income of $ 1.25 as the new benchmark as suggested by the World Bank.

The developed countries of the West have more homogeneity in their populations than the poor countries of the Asia and Africa. In Africa, India and China, there are many heterogeneous groups living in a large numbers of States and provinces. The countries having small territories of land are more amenable to the homogenizing effect of governance than in the case of large countries like India where there are several races, ethnic groups and various regions and sub-social classes. Not all strata in any one society is uniformly aware or informed of their economic, ecological or social statuses, except what is generally available in polls and surveys or what is topically available in bits and pieces in media systems. The general public in these eastern countries are also unaware of the strategies and the ramifications of the policies and programmes instituted by the Governments of these counties. In fact, many Indians are unaware of the lives of the tribals in the north-east part of the country, their beliefs, their sub-cultures and the ways of living.

The heterogeneous groups in the country have their own particular structural arrangements which depict their loyalty ties in a hierarchical system within the parameters of their communities. In social groups, individuals occupy different positions in the hierarchy, formal or informal, in terms of the degree of power for control and decision-making which are components of power. There are some, who are more accomplished than others in leadership, decision-making and management. For example, in the micro family, the patriarch has the greatest power, and in a city, the mayor of the city has greater power than other people in the city. Leadership gives to the leader, power over others who are assumed to be less powerful. This power, however, in the formal structure is bounded by mandates and principles of governance. Those at the helm of governance, whether in the political leadership or the bureaucratic set-up, are expected to show transparency, commitment, responsibility and accountability in their work. Those at the bottom or at the lower end of the society, composed mainly of the poor, are ignorant of the policies and the administrative system of the government. They hardly ever question governmental strategies, and accept them as "givens".

In India, the village, the Block and the District Panchayats are at different levels of hierarchical control. Their goals may be either cohesive or loosely connected in a network that keeps changing as their progressive schemes change through policy and programming as depicted in the Five Year Plans. Such heterogeneous structure is more clearly observable in large countries like China and India than in smaller countries. The nature of interaction is different from the nature of interaction in the bureaucratic and business world. In the latter, it is incumbent upon the leaders to be well-grounded in their profession, whereas in the polity, it can be anyone from any category of people who are able to use diplomacy and the art and craft of control influencing the people.

Where there is homogeneity of goals in the group, the perception of these goals tends to be cohesive. When these goals are not clearly articulated and at times can be flouted, there is usually the lurking expectancy of confrontation, clashes and sometimes dismemberment of the group such as happens in political parties. Occasionally, power might be transferred either by common consent or by the opposition from one group to another. This is exemplified by the changing positions of political groups or parties in countries which follow the parliamentary democratic system as in India. In such systems, several groups vie for the position of the leading Party and many who are aware of which party has the greatest probability to win, will even cross floors. This pattern occurs at election times in the Indian situation. What relevance do the above descriptions have to the poor? The term "power" is exemplified here in many ways in order to show that the poor do not have power and that those who have power over them need not necessarily be business-oriented, nor do they have to be ethical about how they use power. In the political governance in India those who are at the top and hold the power in their hands, usually do so as we have said before to meet their own needs and not necessarily the needs of those who are powerless and poor.

By the term "power", we mean here the significance of the hold or control that a group or a person has over others. This abstract term "power" is operationalised in the action and interaction of the leadership "hub" with the other members of the group who are lower down in terms of power and are subservient to the upper "crust".

Power can be either coercive or persuasive and, according to R. P. French and Bertram Raven, it is to be distinguished from the term influence which is more amorphous and persuasive and not restricted to any one leader or any one goal-direction (French, J. P. R. Jr., and B. Raven, 1960).

Power is a floating ability that is more in some individuals or groups and less in others. For example, a Member of Parliament has more power than a street vendor and a concerted group of parliamentarians can change the course of governance overnight by creating an impasse in the parliamentary system or by confrontation in the progress of parliamentary affairs. Currently, the Indian parliament has a backlog of over 30 Bills waiting to go through the process of law-making by parliamentary procedures. The parliamentary system adopted wholesale from the British is most often manipulated by one party or the other. The conduct of parliamentary affairs and the process of law-making for the good of the people often get delayed by the opposition Members of Parliament in the hues and cries during debates and discussions and thereby causing adjournments. The parliamentarians in India are yet to learn "parliamentary language". Often times, disarray in parliamentary processes occurs motivated by party. They do so by causing concerns rather than programme concerns.

We are not talking of one individual's power over another. Our concern is mainly with political power, which may not be observable, but is cleverly hidden and utilized for the political gains of the opposition. Such situations change dynamically as observable in the case of the current spate of "scams" pertaining mainly to corruption by those who have the power to do so. As for instance, the corruption unearthed in the construction of infrastructure for the Commonwealth Games in Delhi, 2010 and the scam related to 2G spectrum license allocation. Thus, we see the polity by and large is submerged in the interest of the opposition and delays in parliamentary procedures by long spells of debates and arguments. They are like huge bill hoardings along the major streets proclaiming, enhancing, warning and attempting to sell ideas about which there is little known accuracy. For instance, educated and the interested Indian is being bombarded by stories upon stories and still in many cases all that is heard is that "X" has been remanded to custody or that "Y" has been given "bail". The higher-ups tend to promise in placating terms "we will look into the matter and scrutinize the facts", but in the end, as in the case of the famous Bofors scam in the late Eighties, everything is swept under the carpet, trampled upon and forgotten in history.

In this context, we necessarily have to relate political power to economic wealth as economic power can be used for strangling any rumors, whisper- mongering or doing away with whistle blowers. This is not to say that there are Parliamentary members who will always indulge in such devious ways. In fact, there are quite a few upright people in any group, whether politicians or business people, who go by the code of ethics. Take the example of the civic society leaders. They contend that they are committed to fighting for the rights of the poor and so far we have not seen otherwise. Thus, there are both acceptors and rejecters of power.

It is not easy for a civic society group to get answers from authorities in power. The latter will always try to evade or delay the solutions, using subterfuges, in order to gain time to cover up their defaults of indulging in scams and scandals which if they come to light would destroy their power.

The latter scenario is observable in protest rallies where group members collectively protest in a non-violent manner, demanding reversal of laws unfavourable to the general public and especially the poor. This exhibition of power applies also to the situation where State Governments wield their power at will inspite of objections by the Opposition Parties. Labour Unions, for instance, agitate collectively against power holders to seek what they perceive as their right. Such Union display their collectiveness in strikes, in laying down their tools and often paralyzing the operation of functional systems, as had been the case in the crisis in Air India and in some large industries like Maruti Udyog Ltd in 2011. These situations require dialogues and compromises. Such back and forth activities will continue very much like a football game, where no one wins and where it is again "business as usual" whichever or whatever Party or Group is in power.

The recent unraveling of corruption and scams in governance has caused general protests, though peaceful, by the public, mainly with the initiative taken by a a civic society group, to demand redress through the institution of an "Ombudsman-like" authority, namely, a "Lokpal". The power of the collective protest is being felt from time to time like the continuing protests in Kashmir against the arbitrary powers wielded by armed forces, the unrest in the northeast and the demand of farmers for adequate compensation for land acquisitions.

Therefore, power is exerted both by a group of leaders of the people in politics or by the general public themselves without the medium of political representation. The first is usually an institutional power, as in the case of the Parliament, and the second is usually an informal one, collectively put together by the people who are being governed and who find that the governance is not transparent, responsible or accountable in its mandated duties which they are supposed to perform when they take the oath in Parliament.

Therefore, power can be of any type. It may be power to promote the good of the people or to cause and create confusion even to the extent of causing conflict between groups or of calming down what has been a difficult situation. The first kind is that which is given to the leaders in the Government with the understanding that they will perform their duties with special focus on the development of the majority. The second is the type that causes differences within a group as in the North-East part of India and Kashmir, and the third is the type that brings about reconciliation between two or more confronting groups so as to bring about a compromise which has been recently seen in the attempt of the Government to introduce FDI against the uproar of many Parties.

Leadership can be authoritarian or democratic. The kind of leadership we find in some South American and north African countries is authoritarian where there is "one person, one leader" and there are followers irrespective of whether they agree or not with the programmes installed by the leadership. The democratic kind is where everyone and each one has the right to offer his or her opinion freely and over which a consensus takes place. In the Indian parliamentary system, the latter is the usual format and it is for this reason, there is a tendency for a smooth conduct of development activities in contrast to those instituted by an autocratic leader. Autocratic leadership is erratic while the democratic leadership may be predictable.

REFERENCES

Bhalla, G. S., 1994, *Economic Liberalisation and Indian Agriculture*. New Delhi: Institute for Studies in Industrial Development.

French, J. P. R. Jr., and B. Raven, 1960, "The bases of social power", in D. Cartwright and A. Zander (eds.), *Group dynamics*, pp. 607-623. New York: Harper and Row.

Goswami, Rahu, "Why India's 'growth' focus is ignoring the food access question", *Infochange News & Features*, July 2011 at http://infochangeindia.org/agriculture/analysis/why-india-s-growth-focus-is-ignoring-the-food-access-question.html, accessed on 26.12.2011.

Jodhka, S., 2001, *Community and Identities: Contemporary Discourses on Culture and Politics in India*. New Delhi: Sage Publications.

Mathew, George & Baburao Shravan Bhaviskar (eds.), 2009, *Inclusion and Exclusion in Local Governance*. New Delhi: Sage Publications.

Norbu, Dawa, 1996, "Cultural Pre-conditions for development: Tradition and Modernity Reconsidered in the light of Post-Modernism", in Saraswati Baidyanath (ed.), *Interface of Cultural Identity Development*. New Delhi: D.K. Printworld Pvt. Ltd.

Sukhatme, 1965, *Feeding India's Growing Millions*. Bombay: Asia Publishing House.

4

The Relevance of the Indian Parliamentary Democracy for the Poor

India has had a feudal system of governance since times immemorial. At the stroke of midnight on August 15, 1947, it changed to a democratic system under its own rule with all the trappings of a parliamentary democracy based on the model that existed in Great Britain. India borrowed this system wholesale without any preparation of the people as to what the principles implied, how they should be observed, what were the restrictions and privileges and the various ideas and values generated from them. It seems that not only the poor but many of the middle class were not familiar with these principles, nor did they know about the way it was introduced through the Constitution and the way it worked with the help of elections and the functioning of the legislative bodies, both at the Centre and States. The knowledge about the democratic principles rested only with the elite, the upper class and those among the middle class who were educated and knowledgeable and who directly participated in the freedom struggle. As for the poor, they did not have the slightest inkling as to their rights and privileges as laid down in the Constitution. All that they knew was that the *firangis* had left and their country was now being governed by their own people. There was little change in their lifestyle, which was different from that of the country's new leaders. These new leaders of the country were busy in restructuring and setting the parameters of the governance so as to encompass the various heterogeneous groups that composed the country.

Even to this day, over sixty years after Independence, many of those Indians living in far away practically inaccessible areas, including the tribals and nomads, have very little understanding of democracy and are unaware of the various structures of governance and of their rights and privileges guaranteed to them by the Indian Constitution.

The poor in India still continue to have interaction with only the village *panchayat* as the fulcrum of governance. And who speak different ethnic languages. In fact, while the word "Parliament" is called the *Sansad,* the word "democracy", though used as *Prajatantra* in Hindi, is a new term which is not used most often to understand its full meaning even amongst those who are knowledgeable about the Constitution. For the poor majority, representation meant the *Panchayat* and the word Government meant *Sarkar* as used in the days of the old. It stands to reason that the old system of *Jajmani, Jati* and *Jat,* were more comprehensible and translatable into the present day realities. Therefore, nepotism, biased selection, and exchange of favours were familiar context and when continued into the present day regime was still acceptable as usual. Common place incidents in everyday life were acceptable as familiar and therefore the system of giving and taking favours and of indifference towards transgression of civic laws was perceived as acceptable features. For example, people still crossed stop signs at roads, threw garbage on the roadside, and did not think anything of neighbours' behaviour which was against civic norms.

In traditional areas of interaction, the distance between the high and the low castes was still maintained especially in villages. The usual practices like giving the "low" caste workers, who were engaged in menial tasks like sweeping, flaying, tanning and agricultural labour, a glass of *lassi* or few *rotis* was still common. Either class did not enter the other's household. Therefore, this continued feudal practice was a barrier to the poorer "lower" classes who did not think sending children to school as important as working at occupational tasks or farm tasks which were their livelihood. In turn, the *sarkar* still collected tithes and did little maintenance about the village infrastructure as the major concern of the *sarkar* was with the urban structures and systems rather than the rural. Even amongst the poor there were differences in their degree of interaction with the sarkar. The poor in far away villages and tribal areas had less interaction with the *sarkar* than the poor in other rural areas who were closer to urban areas and therefore to the officialdom.

The poor still continue to be beholden to the upper castes, the rich and the powerful politicians as a continuation of the feudal system. Simply put, the *Rajas,* the *Nawabs* and the British have been replaced by people who belonged to their own society. Whether the people standing for election deserved to be elected or not was not the consideration. On the contrary, what was felt as more important was whether those who stood for public office was of their own kind and community. Thus, the voting public seem to be identified with their own ethnic, caste and class groups. The ethics of governance, law and order, are neither understood, nor adhered to. However, strangely enough the poor of the low castes did not or could not elect their own kind because they were too poor to garner votes throughout the community or what is euphemistically called buy votes for cash, because it is well-understood that to stand for a political position implies giving away monies to have oneself elected. The poor of course were out of the scheme of these machinations. All they knew was at the time of the State or general elections they could be paid for voting for politicians in their Constituencies. The main fear in terms of the law and order was that they knew that if they transgressed them, they would be punished by being either fined or put in prison. Therefore, their main attempt was to try and avoid confrontation with the law and to seek the protection of those for whom they voted. This behaviour continues in everyday life as of today. If, for example, there is an accident on the road, people around do not want to render their assistance in the situation, for they do not want to be "involved" as they fear of being dragged into questioning by the police. The sense of citizenry, therefore, was and is, even today, absent in the behaviour of the common people. This is true especially among the poor, for they fear of being involved in to a situation in which they do not know what their rights and privileges are. As the media often reveals, there are cases of certain individuals, who raise the voice of the people with whom they work, being beaten to death. As has happened on one occasion, a man was pulled out of his shop and beaten to death because he did not close his shop during a *Dharna* and the pity of it was that a huge crowd gathered to watch the man being beaten up but did not stretch out a hand to help. Apparently, there are similar cases like this all over the country.

The poor still do not know how to fight for their own rights as they are illiterate, unaware of the principles of the law and how it should be sought for one's own protection. The major tool they use is to walk in groups to protest at the seat of governance (*ahimsa*). They seek the help of their leaders who themselves may be ignorant and have a voice in the governance only by the virtue of being an elected member from the constituency. Moreover, at times of distress among the poor of their constituency, these constituent representatives are hardly in the forefront to fight for them.

This document will not go into details of the system of Parliamentary democracy. Suffice it to say that, as regards the theme of this document, Parliamentary democracy, its privileges and its violations are not understood by the poor. The poor are, so to speak, "led by their noses", leaving them to seek who would best look after their own interests.

As such in the area of their repertoire, all that they know is that there is a large distance between themselves and the so-called government. They are aware that the rich continue to be very rich and that according to karmic laws, they themselves would continue to live the way they were destined to and therefore they are often content with their status. The usual saying was *"jaise hai, vaise hi rahenge"* (would continue to be the same as before); *"yeh, humara karm hai"* (this is our destiny). And for this reason, may be they do not seek opportunities to fight for their own rights and as such they become immune to what is happening far away in the seats of governance. Few know how to read newspapers and still fewer know what to make of television news if they happen to possess one. If they did they would only look at entertainment channel to cheer up their daily life. Again, this is conditioned on whether they have electricity or not as most of the villages in interior remotes areas do not have electricity. The poor are, therefore, was good grist for the mill for the politicians who always wanted to manipulate the people in their constituencies and keep them as least knowledgeable as possible as to what is happening in governance circles around them. So, those who are uneducated and non-knowledgeable continue to be blissfully so.

5

The State of Governance in India

How has India, after more than six decades of freedom, progressed in its developmental programmes? It is well-accepted that during the feudal and colonial days, the poor were in the main forgotten, and so were most of the middle class in urban areas. The political power during feudal and colonial days was especially functional for increasing the power of the favourite classes of the rulers, namely, the Rajas and the *Nawabs*. The pre-colonial ruling powers were most of the time occupied with territorial wars and paid little attention to the development of the poor. At the village level, the rulers were only interested in the collection of "tithes" ("*lagaan*") through their agents called *patwaris*. If tithes were paid, the agriculturists who held small poor joint landholdings and had to pay these taxes, could barely exist. The plight of the sharecroppers and the casual labourers who were paid in kind was even more unpredictable and dismal.

It is naïve to think that India's Independence movement was just an anti-British struggle. When the movement gained strength and wider public support, it rode mainly on the slogans of freedom from poverty and progressive change in the lifestyles of the vast majority of the people. The "land to the tiller" was one of the important slogans during the Independence movement. In fact, the decisive push to the national movement against colonial rule came with the large scale peasant mobilization towards the later part of the freedom movement (Anand Kumar, 2003). The various manifestations of people's protests against an unjust social system were also assimilated into the independence movement. These included protests of the social categories that were historically disadvantaged and deprived such as the "untouchable" castes that now come under the rubric of "Scheduled Castes". Because of these characteristics of the freedom movement, it was logical that the Constitution framed for governing a free India proclaimed in its Preamble the principles of *Justice, Equality* and *Fraternity* as its major tenants of governance. Apparently, these were high sounding concepts imitated from the Anglo-Saxon rulers. In India, only a few among the intelligentsia understood the meaning of these terms. The general population at large, hidden away in tribal forests, desert lands and remote rural areas, little understood the import of these concepts as their relationship to their lifestyles was not comprehensible to them.

In the efforts of leading the country towards the path to modernisation and development, independent India instituted the mechanism of Five Year Plans for development. In the first Five Year Plan under the Nehru regime, agricultural development received priority over industrial development. But all that happened in agriculture was that the production and productivity increased due to the introduction of the Mexican short-stub wheat variety. However, it did not happen that land was allotted to the sharecroppers, and more importantly, the landless poor. Thus, the programme of what was euphemistically called the Green Revolution could benefit only those large farmers who could afford new agricultural inputs and technology.

During the time of Lal Bahadur Shastri, the White Revolution or the technology of processing milk and milk products from the villages began in Anand in Gujarat which became successful, in that there was a wider distribution of the Amul products, the brand name given to the dairy products.

During the period of Indira Gandhi's regime, there was a tighter hold on the reforms of the economic structure, especially in relation to the expansion of credit directed towards the less-abled among the poorer agriculturists who were given subsidized agricultural amenities. It was during Indira Gandhi's regime that there was a shift in focus towards the poor with such programmes as the 'Twenty Point Programme', '*Garibi Hatao*', subsidies to poor farmers and the development of slums in urban areas. After her regime and during the short period of Rajiv Gandhi's rule, these programmes for the poor continued but gradually fell into disuse because of the increasing corruption of power by the politicians in connivance with the bureaucracy and the corporate world. Since then the politicians became more astute and covert in the art of nepotism and favoritism and in taking cuts as commissions for the allocation of project licenses and tenders to the bribe-giving corporate world. Thus, the budgetary allocations were partially siphoned off by the artful middlemen, who, on the one hand, represented the people in the constituencies, but, on the other hand, nevertheless found their way to "covert cuts". The regimes that ensued concentrated on industrialisation and technology development in which the control and stakes were exclusively with the rich, while the poor continued to remain poor.

The major policies implemented, besides the developmental programs of the Five Year Plans, were related to the uplift of women, care of children and the socially disadvantaged groups of Scheduled Castes and Scheduled Tribes. The programmes meant for these vulnerable sections of people have been poorly implemented. It is well-known that the passing of Bills in Parliament are usually token gestures. There are gross inadequacies in the management, implementation, monitoring and evaluation of such welfare and developmental programmes. Bureaucrats who were and still are in charge of the programmes hardly visit the field of action. Politicians usually attended the inaugural events of such programmes but hardly showed any earnest interest in their progression except the related desk jobs involved in planning and the relevant evaluation programmes. These were desk jobs far removed from the sites.

Corporate houses install charitable institutions to appear as benefactors of the poor, but actually to avoid taxation. However, the poor still continue to be isolated from the genuine interest of their constituency overlords. The bureaucrats who are in control at the district level and the Pradhans in villages are totally in command and could manipulate the implementation of programmes, especially when they are armed with the knowledge of how to bypass the policies at the ground level concentrating mainly on enlarging their own pockets.

Community Development Programmes

It is important here to talk in detail about the community development programmes, because it was the first and it spearheaded the emphasis on the participation of people in their development in a holistic manner and was given the title "community development programme". The major focus was on training the participants in taking command over their own projects for development, using better inputs so as to get higher yields.

One of the first programmes for rural development and poverty eradication was based on community development. Community development existed long before it was re-formulated by the independent India in 1952. The government thought it was wise to take to the Panchayati Raj System as its modular structure to re-mould development programmes suitable to the hitherto neglected poor in the hinterlands of whom the colonists took little notice of except to gather tithes from the agriculturists for their revenues. The Panchayat as is well-known was composed of selected leaders of the village who came together for purposes of settlement of differences and arriving at decisions as a whole. Simple strategies were used in this structure. The Indian government thought it would be more useful to use a familiar structure and introduced a hierarchical ladder of the panchayat system, namely, at the village level, called the *Gram Sabha,* at the Block level, called the Block *Panchayat,* and further at the District level, called the District Panchayat. Together they formed a number of hierarchically arranged representative local bodies from the village to district level. These government agents were expected to help implement plan programs and strategies which were compatible with the informal structures at each level. The District Collectors were the overall representatives of the Government at the district level. Planning was done at each level as suited to the needs of the area, namely, village, block and district. The panchayats were helped to develop their own plan under the budgetary allocations given to them, assisted and overseen by block development officers, so that there was a connection between the district, the block and the village in terms of cohesion of developmental activities.

Communities in India covered a whole range of descriptive identities which have their own unique characteristics apart from others. Nevertheless, communities exist side by side maintaining these parameters. Some of them, over time, have higher statuses than the others and hence had more power. In the management of these groups together, it was essential that there were leaders and there were followers and as such the politics of status came into being where one had more power over the other and could wield its influence to systematize the other less powerful adjoining communities, while each group maintained its identity apart from the other (Sujata, Patel, 2001).

The major objective of the *Panchayati Raj* system was to encourage people's participation at the local level. It was thought that the participants should feel that each programme was their own for which they were also responsible. In a sense this was supposed to be decentralized local planning and execution of programs that met the needs of the local people and yet reflected the parameters of developmental planning for each year under the aegis of the Five Year Plans. Revenues were collected through the formal agency of the government which also distributed credit and subsidies as determined according to the planned strategies and, in turn, the parallel government hierarchy of officials was expected to monitor and evaluate the progress of the projects at the ground level.

Since the community development programme is the fulcrum of rural development, the Government of India thought it significant enough in 1993 to institute a set of Constitutional reforms, through the Constitution 73rd Amendment. This was for decentralization of power and for instituting local self governments at the district, sub-district and panchayat levels. Through this method, the Government gave most of the powers of development to the leaders of the panchayat which they hoped would also encourage more of the community people to be involved in the development strategies. In many of these local panchayats, women representatives were also involved so as to represent women's problems. Naturally, the first priority was agricultural development and towards this end, agricultural universities in each State were set up by the Ministry of Food and Agriculture. This was according to the model developed in the United States where each department through its extension wings would go out into rural areas to help institute new ideas on farm and household management. Besides this, each department in the university also had wings of research and innovative modular programmes which were experimented in several villages. Such research were undertaken to develop improved seeds, fertilizers and pesticides in order to increase farm yield, both in terms of the quality and quantity. The institutes also undertook innovative methods of farming.

Craig Johnson (2003) in his paper analyzing the experience of the States of Andhra Pradesh and Madhya Pradesh in the decentralization process observed that both these States had great variation and diversity in their experience, which reflected their own unique mix of colonial administration, feudal legacy and agrarian transition. However, three elements continue to act as barriers to the realization of this decentralization. The first is the federal umbrella; the second was the heavy resistant bureaucracy and the third the elitist segments in the decentralized ambit. While it appeared that policies might change the flavour and direction of new farming methods, the holistic efforts of the university, the local extension divisions and the movement towards integrating house and farm would yield better results. These development programmes, however, did not take into account those who were non-agriculturists who continued to live their marginalized life as before.

Besides the theme of local self-governance, social historicity is an important factor in the analysis of village life. Three factors may be abstracted. This analysis centers on classification into social groups at the caste level, sub-caste level, and family and kinship level, the latter being the microcosm of the total village society (Khan, H. Iltija, 1967). Viewed from another perspective, this is a reflection of the old system of Jati and *Jajmani* analysed by Carstairs (1957) several decades ago.

The community development programme as it existed since Independence has unfortunately not been analysed in terms of the base that it has already existed upon, namely, do the local people at the village level employ their own group, either family or kin group or caste? More often than not this perception did not go beyond caste to include other castes and other unknown groups that settled down from time to time in the area. In actual fact, the community in the community development paradigm implies the whole community contained in a village, in a block and in a district. This perception did not exist in the average villager's mind and, therefore, the word participation did not imply that he should be involved in the whole process and in time the programme itself developed into an idea that it was assistance given to them by the government officials and was a sarkari programme. As such the total decentralization process had little meaning in terms of self-participation and, therefore, the whole apparatus continued to have the same rigid parameters as before. The government was continued to be perceived as a charity-giving organization to obtain which the villager did not have to interact, make decisions or participate in the community development programmes (Khan, H. Iltija, 1967). In India, the community development programme which began a little after the declaration of independence and was ideally thought to be the best way of pulling together the various heterogeneous trends of little communities was hastily ill-perceived and implemented because the people themselves were not socially or educationally prepared. They were just thrust into the programs on the basis of the perceptions of the leaders. These leaders, it must be underscored, had most of the training in urban universities, whether in India or abroad. Pandit Nehru, Gandhi ji, Vallabh Bhai Patel and Muhammad Ali Jinnah, all went to foreign universities. India at that time comprised the areas of the present Pakistan and Bangladesh, besides its own sizeable mainly Hindu population. Therefore, the same social fabric remained in India as it did in the divided Pakistan and Bangladesh. These divisions are on the basis of religion so that those who constituted Hindu India were mainly those who belonged to the Hindu religion and a few of the other religions who preferred to remain in India while Bangladesh and Pakistan were mainly Muslim. The homogeneous religious groups in India were not sufficiently conversant with the ideology of community development through the community. It took a long time for agricultural development to take place in India. Technology seems to have favoured only the rich farmers who could afford to buy tractors and threshers and improved seed varieties.

It is found that local participation can be successful dependent upon the competencies within the community which are not self-centered. For example, the State of Kerala is an outstanding example of the community holding together in terms of participatory development, not only of the upper echelons but all the way down to the marginalized. Participation had existed for a long time in this State which had communism as its basis and, therefore, the ethic continued to be unitary in perception for the common good of the common people. Perhaps, local decentralization, given its rightful place in the development process and educated awareness have served to enhance the spirit of participation in this State unlike other States such as Bihar, Madhya Pradesh and Rajasthan which have been affected by segregated communities which are unable to hold together as one community in participatory self-governance. Further, such poor States do not have the educated awareness of working together for the common good of their own.

What perhaps operates the variability of this togetherness is the perception that education is essential for understanding and implementing services and structures that benefit the total village, including the low castes. This does not mean that the divisiveness disappears, but that the perception of it is reduced in the institutional framework of self-governance. The poor in the northern States of Bihar, Orissa, and Madhya Pradesh and UP will continue to protect its divisiveness so long as there is lack of educated awareness that development proceeds on a holistic basis and not just in segmented sections of the society. The major reason for this divisiveness is that the polity and bureaucracy is aware that these states have the largest number of uneducated naïve people who have not fully understood the essence of the change in the polity of the country from colonialism to democracy. They, therefore, continue to behave in the same old ways as they did during the feudal and colonial days, perceiving their own political leaders as they did the previous masters.

From the inception of the community development programme, the basic premise has been the inclusion of the people themselves, mainly the beneficiaries, as participants in their own programmes. There was a misconceived idea that by naming the community people as participants would automatically give them a sense of commitment to the totality of the wellbeing of the total community. There was little realization that the programme targeted mainly agriculturists and left out the non-agriculturists who were actually the needier of the two and that the programme also favoured the upper castes rather than the lower castes. Unfortunately, the Government chose to have its own bureaucratic representatives for the implementation of the programme. It is well-known that the Government officers and workers were paid employees and were not as committed as voluntary organizations, simply because the latter volunteers were spontaneously interested and were genuinely committed to programmes. Further, the word community implies a large number of people of heterogeneous variety living and working together in conjunction with common goals, whereas the Government mistakenly thought that this programme would involve all members of a heterogeneous variety. It is reasonable to assume that when we disassemble the word community, in the Indian context, it implies different castes, different creeds and different ethnic groups living together as heterogeneous little communities. Therefore, in enveloping all as a homogeneous community did not really affect the real poor target group to the extent that it should have. The latter were relatively naïve about the benefits they should get since they were at the lowest rung of the caste groups and were self-effacing. It was but natural that the Government employees would work relatively easily with the upper castes, with the political leaders and the influential that were higher ups in the bureaucracy rather than the poor who were mostly casual labourers. Over time, the benefits of the produce were grabbed by the articulate better off sections of the community giving a poor pittance to the needier lower castes, who were the hidden group and the least knowledgeable. For this reason, several evaluations showed that while the community development programme really ought to have focused on the relatively poorer sections of the society, it was easier for them to show results by interacting with and helping the more articulate and better off of the social groups. In time, the poor castes began to feel that they were being given charity by the government and, therefore, were grateful receivers without having to participate in the programme. This marginalization of the really needy was further reflected in the follow-on developmental programmes where the paradigms were more or less the same, but were given different titles. Therefore, there was little new that was happening except some trickle-down effect for the poor in the community.

There is a great deal of debate on inclusion and exclusion of different castes in the development programmes such as the lower castes, the Adivasis, the poor Muslims and females. How much was attuned to their needs and how much to those who held the whip in the conduct of development programmes and, therefore, its budgetary allocations, is still not clear. Since community development implied a totality of individuals in the targeted area, all through the various castes and occupations, the concentration was really on the agriculturists since increase in produce was a priority factor. Democracy could not work as expected since there was a hiatus between the knowledge of the better off and those of the marginalized as to the meaning of development, community participation and a "togetherness" spirit (Alam, Javed, 2010). For these reasons, the fields and the habitats of the better off were much more well-cared for in terms of structures and facilities than the areas where the marginalized lived and worked.

The Government workers should have been well-trained to reinforce the poor to make them feel as participants in executing the programmes, as well as given them power and authority to implement the programmes. All along the line of bureaucracy from the district collector to the block development officer and the village level worker, there was no particular interest in the community participating in the programme as if it were their own. To the target group, it was the government that was doing the work for them and, therefore, there was a non-commitment on their part to take initiatives. While the target group took very little interest in activities meant for them, many committed NGOs who stayed with them like SEWA and the programme at Tilonia urged the participants to own their own achievements.

Participation of women in this programme was relatively poor except in some cases of village panchayats where women were also represented. Women in poor agricultural households or in casual labour households tend to move with their men-folk to cities in search of casual labour, indicative of their powerlessness and poverty-driven migration (Sadhna, Arya & Roy Anupama, 2006).

Even after the introduction and the continuance of the community development programme, when Indira Gandhi came into power, other programmes were introduced such as "Eradication of Poverty" (*Garibi Hatao*) and other rural development and poverty eradication programmes like the Integrated Rural Development Programme (IRDP), and support to small-scale enterprises. The goals of these programmes are still not even tangentially realized. Except for the Integrated Child Develoment Scheme (ICDS) which has become an elephantine Balwadi programme, others have more or less faltered along the way. The latest programme for poverty eradication, namely, the Mahatma Gandhi National Rural Employment Guarantee Scheme, is still in its founding stages and perhaps fumbling. Its future progress, however, is yet unknown.

The Integrated Rural Development Programme (IRDP) was initiated in 1979. The aim of this programme was to help the rural poor to acquire assets for engaging in income-generating micro-enterprises and thus to enable them to cross the poverty line. It was termed integrated as it attempted to offer both low-interest micro credit through banks and subsidies from the government in the purchase of assets. By the end of 1994, the total cumulative outlay had grown to Rs. 132 billion in credit and Rs. 82 billion in subsidy (Copestake, James G., 1996). However, as with all gigantic ill-managed programmes, there were many loop-holes. In an evaluation study of this programme by Osmani, it was found that 24 per cent of assets did not generate any income and another 50 per cent of the assets did not make any contribution to the net disposable income of the families (Osmani, S. R., 1990). This example illustrates the inefficiency and perhaps corrupt practices in distribution and management at the ground level and more especially the lack of awareness of the target group of their entitlements. The utilization of monies was often delayed as the process got entangled in inefficient management by poorly trained government personnel.

It was mostly the rich borrowers who through political maneuvering were the major beneficiaries. The poor had no adequate debt-capacity. Though subsidies offered by the Government could have compensated for this, the corrupt practices of lower functionaries of the scheme saw to it that the better off people who were above the poverty-line could manipulate to get the subsidies and loans, depriving the really needy the benefits of this programme (N. C. Saxena). Besides, although the interest rates of bank loans were low, the poor beneficiaries had to pay out-of pocket expenses and payment to middlemen thus raising the effective interest rate very high and unaffordable for them (Mahajan, Vijay, and Bharti Gupta Ramola, 1996). Thus, the whole concept and design of the IRDP was not well-planned and enacted to reach the really needy poor. Neither was it planned and implemented in an integrated manner nor did it employ a holistic concept of development as a package. Moreover, credit and loan-giving was not on a continuous basis, which led to the attritioning of the efforts of the borrower. The programme neglected to conduct the pre-project planning assessment in knowing what the actual priority needs of the needy were. Their priorities were mainly in terms of consumption needs such as for the household food and for healthcare. In terms of evaluation, perhaps one in five benefited from this program. Inadequate administrative appraisal and the interference of the political system greatly deflected the goals of the program. It still remains a fumbling large and inadequately implemented programme.

The *Jawahar Rozgar Yojna* that followed was another scheme which attempted to help the poorest of the poor. Data indicate that the unemployed rural people were about 4.3 per cent at the time of the implementation of this programme in 1989, while 8.7 per cent were said to be under-employed. These figures usually do not take into account the casual labourers. The number of casual labourers were said to be much more marked in rural areas where employment, as is well-known, is seasonal. Therefore, off-farm employment opportunities required special provision of governmental assistance. As agriculture became more technologized, the demand for manpower diminished which affected the poorest illiterate labourers the most and the rural families became even more marginalized. For these reasons of lack of constant employment for the poor, the two existing programs, namely, National Rural Employment Program (NREP) and Rural Landless Employment Guarantee Programme (RLEGP) were merged into *Jawahar Rozgar Yojna* (JRY) in 1989-90. The programme, as usual, deployed a large rhetoric of objectives such as: alleviation of poverty through supplementary employment opportunities for the rural poor during agricultural slack periods, increasing agricultural wage rates and creating social assets such as roads and school buildings and organisation of the poor through public participation (Raghav Gaiha, P. D. Kaushik and Vani Kulkarni, 1998).

The Planning Commission's evaluations of this programme, however, indicated successful utilization of the budget and an increase in man working days. But it is well-known that governmental reports arising from field level staff usually show exaggerated figures and such like discrepancies. So, "the truth is still out there" as these figures did not have any basis of reliability. The executors, managers and evaluators were recast from the same mould as before. This resulted in the better off being more able to cream off the benefits than did the poorest of the target group. Both the political leadership and the bureaucracy were hand in glove in proclaiming the success of the programme. The concurrent evaluations, by and large, showed a great deal of disparity between the amount allocated for man-days of employment and the actual employment in operation. In some states, the utilization was less than expected, and there is little information about the funds utilized by the panchayats which as a whole were in charge of development programmes at the field level. The major drawback was that all this monumental data gathering and data reporting was unreliable in the main, and the data gathered were not utilized in the modification of the programme parameters for the future.

In tribal developmental programmes, there was also a misconception and at times mismanagement. Very little attention was paid to tribals living in forest areas. Many tribes who live on forest produce needed specific assistance for development. There is a wrong understanding that tribals are only forest produce utilizers and do not add to its re-furbishing. Not many attempts have been made to understand the psyche of the tribals who have maintained their geo-ecological habitat for generations. They are not only consumers but are also aware of afforestation and preservation. Forest dwellers are careful to maintain their forests by re-sowing and maintaining the wooded environment which they have done for the past generations. Those who live in the upper regions of the snowline mountains maintain themselves by living on the produce of their ice-bound areas by catching fish, seals and such like, being careful not to destroy their reproduction, and preserving them for consumption during the winter months. Thus, they preserve their ecological habitat.

In actual fact, forests and forest produce in tribal areas are being denuded by industrialists who buy their lands at cheap prices for expanding their industrial base. It is reported that about 100 million forest dwellers in the country live in and around forest lands, and another 275 million live of the produce of the forest (Sankaran, Kamala; Shalini Sinha and Roopa Madhav, 2012). Non-Timber Forest Products are a source of survival for many tribals and where timber is abundant some are utilized for sale to middlemen so as to obtain food and other essentials for survival. Over-exploitation of forest resources for industrial, infrastructural and other development projects and the consequent destruction of forest ecologies have forced many tribal communities to leave their traditional ways of life and their natural habitat and venture out to the plains, remote towns and cities in search of uncertain livelihood means. They are therefore dispossessed of their rightful ecology. For example, the basket weavers of Karnataka found that they were faced with exhaustion of bamboo growth in the forests, jeopardizing their very livelihood as basket weavers and therefore reducing their means for livelihood. Thus, forest tribals are in a distressed condition because of the growing technology of the powerful industrialists overpowering them.

The Indian Constitution provides for protection of rights in land for Scheduled Tribes, but the laws made by the Indian state in the name of facilitating development through dams, industrial and mining projects, have only accelerated the dispossession of lands of the tribals. Land for land as compensation is generally not provided and empirical studies point out that displacement has led to large increase in extents of landlessness among the tribals. It has also resulted in cultural, social and economic dislocations for tribals (Kumar, Kundan; Pranab Ranjan Choudhary; Soumendra Sarangi, Pradeep Mishra, Sricharan Behera, 2005). A case in point is that of Kucheipadar village of Raigarh district in Orissa. The government in 1992 sanctioned mining project to Utkal Alumina International Limited (UAIL). The tribals found that there was no response to their appeal to stop the mining industry from encroachment into their living habitat from both the government and the company officials. Hence, they organized themselves into *Prakutika Sampada Suraksha Parishad* (PSSP) or Council for Protection of Natural Resources. After many protest rallies, on 15 December 2000, there was a confrontation between the Parishad and the state police where several of the tribals were killed. This forced the company to reduce its mining activities and simultaneously build a rehabilitation colony. Therefore, the issue is not about tradition versus modernization, whereas, it is more about freedom from control by outsiders and to allow forest-dwellers to live their lifestyles as did their forefathers. Inspite of all protests by the tribals, the state continued to support the company as it brought in revenue for the state which was hand-in-hand with the mining overlords in Orissa. This modernizing activity of mining for capital formation is in reality stealing the poor tribals to facilitate the money-making activities of the urban rich and powerful (Patibandla Srikant, 2009). Currently the same story raises its head in the States of Karnataka and Andhra Pradesh where mining capitalists extract iron ore illegally, helped by the connivance of politicians and bureaucrats, which is now turned into a scam.

The Position of Women

Given the general disadvantaged conditions of women and the fact that most of them are illiterate and overburdened with household chores, the female is the least considered and the most excluded, and the most exploited from the community development parameters. The female is the most hard-worked, doing both agricultural labour as well as domestic chores, estimated at 14 hours a day (Davaer, B.D., 1995). If we talk about an enlightened household, the first priority is an enlightened mother and daughter which does not usually occur in the poor households. If a mother was not educated and enlightened, it had an adverse effect on the children in terms of their learning skills and educational opportunities. As is well-known, in traditional families, the patriarch hardly interacts in household chores. This distance between the patriarch and the child further isolates the child in terms of his or her ability to gain more than book knowledge. This lack of reinforcement, therefore, depletes the need to achieve. Children from such poor families tend to follow the same occupation as their fathers did, thereby accounting for the large number of children working as child labourers in agriculture.

Therefore, we have observed from the detailing of developmental programmes directed mainly towards the rural areas that they have not succeeded to the extent expected. Perhaps, the problem lies in the growing numbers of people every year due to the growing rate of population growth in rural areas. Also, the problem may be due to a lack of accurate knowledge of how monies are spent, whether to the farmer or non-farmer. We have also observed that in order to deliver services in the form of cash or ration cards or money-subsidies or unemployment benefits, there is often a lack of knowledge at the administrative levels about how the monies should be spent at the field level, whether the right amount of subsidized inputs have been given or have been short-changed by the agents at the field-level. For instance, it is not feasible for the Government to give poor farmers pesticides and insecticides when their land is not fertile and when there is no proper irrigation facilities, especially, during the non-monsoon period. Therefore, how do we know about the proper distribution of facilities and subsidies unless there is transparent management and monitoring by the field agents?

India being a very large country requires a heavy input of trained and committed personnel. It is well known that individuals who are in permanent government jobs tend to be slack in the output of their work and depend mainly upon record-keeping and writing of reports.

While it is admitted that agricultural inputs are given directly to the farmer, the level of consumption of food and other basic items rests in the hands of the women of the household. If cash inputs have to be given as in the National Rural Employment Guarantee Scheme, there is no surety that the money from the scheme would be utilized for the benefit of the family. It has been suggested that cash should go directly to the female of the household through rural banks, except that the dilemma is that the females do not know how to conduct the paper work or what they should do when they deal with banks. Therefore, females need to be trained in the process of bank transactions. For this reason, a huge training programme is required for assisting in household situation for household food security purposes.

Where there is credit financing, some leeway exist in saying that the subsidies like food from ration shops and subsidising of female entrepreneurial activities are well-utilized by the female themselves. Further, it is expected that incentives for female householders will attract children to attend school continuously.

After elaborate analysis, the Planning Commission has stated that Rs. 32 per day in urban areas and Rs. 26 per day in rural areas were adequate for a person to exist on. This limit would then give information as to really how many live below the poverty line (BPL). Unfortunately, with the price index being erratically up and down these would seem to be non-reliable figures.

Again, we must admit that these are assessments made from time to time on the basis of desk work and at the ground level it is not very clear as to who is really poor and who is really above the poverty line since practices related to food and its consumption depend upon many other changes in the community and production.

It would be better if the food subsidies in kind are given to the household families directly. Although the PDS does exist, it is not doing well as many of the ration shops deliberately do not supply everything that is needed by the households on the basis of ration cards. If the female has money in her hand, she can buy whatever ration she needs. This will prompt shopkeepers to have ready stocks available in their shops so that they are able to sell on a monetary basis and not restricted to the ration-card system. The above are suggestions which may or may not work as each community varies one from the other. But, experiments need to be tried out in order to assess whether they work or not. On the other hand, there is some concern that if the PDS is removed, it will lead to unintended consequences such as further rise in prices of food items, which will defeat the purpose of food security (Dreze, Jean, 2011).

The debate may have to centre around issues like: What will be the extent of budgetary allocations if the BPL is raised to a higher limit and how this higher allocation will be utilized. Therefore, logically these amounts are just estimates on the basis of statistical knowledge of availability of money at the household level, which will change from time to time: It is well known that this estimate of the Planning Commission may only be indicative. The issue is what is the agreed upon basic amount essential for survival, and as to whether it is available to the poor. It is also important to indicate the source of this money or its equivalent in essential items of consumption. Has it subsided totally or partially, or is it just some abstract analysis? Naturally, if thc family is living on farming, wheat or other produce of the land owned by the family has to be accounted for in the income of the family as it is a staple food from their very own farm, but if the family is one of casual labourers, the family has to buy everything to provide for itself. The more realistic objective is to provide job opportunities in the rural areas, so that people earn their own livelihood, while farmers utilize the subsidies in a proper manner. This calls for a huge overhaul of the subsidy-cum-financing-cum-unemployment benefit programmes. How much will this accrue to, and given the spiraling costs of food items, will it be easier to notate changes in the BPL as the consumer price index changes. This is not an easy problem to tackle as the area of distribution is far beyond the means of number of personnel to undertake this distribution of government subsidies, credits and other items and to monitor the utilization of the BPL cards. We require a few simple direct methods for reaching the poor. Therefore, a more realistic paradigm shift is required in order to more nearly assess the BPL families. The paradigm should shift from the occupational levels to the household levels. It is suggested that the following measures may be examined as to their implementation:-

(1) Subsidies and credit for farmers should be in the form of actual material so that the money will not be diverted to other expenditures.
(2) Money for household food security should be handed over directly to the females of the household from an institutional base, and
(3) It is essential that the future generation, namely, the current day children, even while they are studying, should also learn some technical occupations which will be useful after school for earning and adding to the family income.

India is going forward rapidly in terms of technology and trade and, therefore, it is essential that the country reduces the number of below poverty line households, so that individuals can earn a decent standard of living. All attempts should be made to free children from labour and encourage them to complete the schooling while correspondingly teaching them technical and mechanical skills. More emphasis should be given to technical education after school, rather than going to colleges to simply complete a bachelor's degree. With the facilities available of the open school and universities like the Indira Gandhi National Open University, individuals especially youngsters can work and simultaneously study further so that not only are they educated but also have technical skills to seek and maintain jobs.

Indices of consumer price are an important estimate of poverty. The main index of the price rise for industrial workers is measured by CPIIW (Consumer Price Index for Industrial Workers) and for agricultural workers by CPIAL (Consumer Price Index for Agricultural Labourers) (Deaton, Angus & Alessandro Tarozzi, 2000). India contributes more people to world poverty than any other country.

Because of the length of base in time of using these two indices and amount of weightage accruing to them, it was thought better to use commodity level prices weighted using the more recent and more poverty-relevant weights. The use of information from the NSSO survey of prices is an innovative way of finding the poverty-related consumer price index. Therefore, the combination of rise in consumer index and the rise in prices of the commodities together with expenditure levels form a more cohesive perspective on the state of poverty. It is possible that the calculations of urban poverty is on the lower side as there is no support from the NSSO data for the argument that urban prices are much higher than rural prices. The use of NSSO data provides a useful basis for calculating inter-state differences in CPIIW and CPIAL (Deaton, Angus & Alessandro Tarozzi, 2000).

The inequality between rural and urban poverty has been because of the migration of rural people from rural to urban areas, which gives rise to further inequality between the rural and the urban. Further, the differences in relation to the higher earnings from the industrialized urban areas vis-à-vis the agrarian rural areas affect this indexing. Economic growth also seems to have increased regional variations. Inequality adds to the differentiations in the growth rate. Inclusive growth of the economy seems to be the best bet to reduce these differences. The increase in tax revenue, the better attention paid to agricultural growth and the inclusion of the non-economic social variables will lead to a more sustainable development perspective and, therefore, more stability in the irrevocable shifts in growth and equality (Jha, R., 2000).

From the above inferences about economic growth, polity and poverty, we find that by and large there is only a marginal fall in poverty. This is so especially in rural areas and now with the rise of consumer price index, the purchasing power of the poor has dwindled down considerably. We might, therefore, assume that when the figures are postulated for 2009 and 2012, the status of variables indexing poverty like hunger, malnutrition, less access to clean drinking water and other necessities are also affected. This may also be due to the incapacity of the poor in rural areas to sustain themselves as their mainstay is in agrarian development. This is so because liberalisation and globalization for the agriculturists have received lesser attention than industry and technology. This decreases the urban poverty in comparison to rural poverty. It is said that out of every rupee spent on poverty alleviation programs, only 15 paise reaches the target group. The privatization that accompanies the liberalisation and globalization has the effect of increasing the costs of shelter, clothing and other essential needs of lighting and water.

However, solutions are not as simple as giving rural banks the responsibility for credit financing. The whole process is fraught with loopholes. In recent years, there has been an emphasis on micro financing for the poor. This is done by the creation of regional and rural banks to facilitate services for the poor as they have been excluded from the formal financial system. The tasks of micro-finance are to promote greater financial inclusion and, in the process, improve the social and economic welfare of the poor. However, the National Sample Survey Organization's (NSSO), 59th Round (2003) revealed that only 48.6 per cent of the poor received credit from both formal and informal sources (financial inclusion in a broader sense) and the remaining 51.4 per cent did not receive any credit (total financial exclusion). However, 22 per cent of the cultivator households received credit from informal sources. Further, a World Bank survey, 2003, revealed that 79 per cent of the rural households had no access to credit from formal sources. Therefore, the suggestion that making the female the recipient of credit does not still solve the problem as large numbers are excluded from the ambit of macro financing through institutional services. The basic conclusion of the above information is that the purpose to 'include the excluded' is still not satisfactory to the extent expected (Naveen K Shetty, 2008). In accruing the benefits of micro-financing to the poor, there are some barriers. These barriers are: lack of assets, physical weakness, isolation, vulnerability and powerlessness.

It is said that in India the numbers of people living under the poverty line has risen to 40 crores. This is based on the definition of poverty line adopted by India's planning Commission. There is much controversy on this subject as it is argued that this "line" will keep shifting and, therefore, the amount necessary for living above or below the poverty line since these depend upon the consumer price index which fluctuates from time to time. The majority of programs for poverty alleviation assume that the beneficiaries are aware of their political rights and privileges.

Unfortunately the poor lack this knowledge. Also, poverty alleviation by the system of micro-financing is not fully known to the poor as the poor are neither educated nor knowledgeable (D Rajashekhar, 2004). Further, the potential of microfinance to contribute to reduction in poverty is suspect. So far, the impact of this credit system has been evaluated only in terms of the financial success and performance of these micro-level financial institutions and not in terms of the impact on the lives of the clients of these institutions, namely, the poor who are in need of such subsidized credit (Alok Misra, 2006).

We have described above in detail several factors that deter the progress of the marginalized and the lack of full commitment by governance. Added to these are factors which are more potent like political maneuvering in the process of distribution, management, monitoring and evaluation of how subsidies are utilized.

Apart from the Government, there are many NGOs in the field of development work. NGOs are non-governmental organisations which have existed even before India became independent. During the colonial period several missionaries in the form of non-governmental organisations came to India to offer charity, education and also to attempt to proselytize or to convert the poor to Christianity. The potential converts, who were mainly from the lower castes and people in tribal areas, were ready to receive whatever help came in their way and in their own naïve fashion accepted the package of help, becoming in the bargain fervent Christians. In time, several NGOs were formed by philanthropic Indians themselves who looked into different issues like poultry-keeping, weaving, arts and crafts and whatever was the potential of a given community. These NGOs lived with the participants in their own areas, so that the activities were genuine and in earnest and bore fruit. Later on, several NGOs from different organisations or those which were initiated by the civic society came forward to help the fragile and the poor in many enterprises. Some of them have been in existence for a long time but have not produced outstanding work. They are more or less organisations which install general programmes. Many of the NGOs are self-located in geo-ecological areas where they have an expertise and where they feel they can contribute to the community goals, for instance, in watershed management, as in the work of Tarun Bharat Sangh in

Alwar District, Rajasthan; women's entrepreneurial work, as in Tilonia, Rajasthan; and such like small-scale efforts related to small communities. Therefore, they are scattered in such a fashion that a total perspective is not available in relation to a particular enterprise. For instance, some prefer to work with tribals in teaching of certain skilled arts so as to increase their income. Some others coordinate the work of tribals and help them manage sales such as in Yellamanchali in Andhra Pradesh who work with community on a commercial basis to sell their product of leaf. Plates for the use of temple, and still others live with the community to help them tackle the totality of the wellbeing of the community. When the volunteers of NGOs live with the communities themselves, their output is more successful and more steadfast than when there are NGOs who visit these communities from time to time and help them in some rather insignificant areas, which really have no lasting benefits. Therefore, much depends upon the willingness of the NGOs to live at the ground level with the community. At times this is difficult because many NGOs work on a voluntary basis and are hardly paid. However, there are others who pay themselves very well from the funds they collect but hardly work at the ground level with the people, especially when the latter are extremely poor because it requires a great deal of inputs to lift the poor above their poverty line, especially when the work has to be directed towards the most fragile in the population, namely, young children and females. More often, the NGOs are merely registered bodies with little assets and families. It is dubious as to how much of success they can bring about when they are not constantly in touch with the community they proclaim to work for. CAPART, which monitors the work of most rural NGOs, has blacklisted many of the NGOs which have hardly any output to show as success. These NGOs being voluntary have to procure funds and may not have constant and consistent funds to carry on their work and, therefore, there are many stoppages in their work for the communities. Procurement of funds is a constant bugbear and irregular in terms of the length of the time the projects are funded. When the funding period is over, it is but natural that the work dries up and there is no self-sustenance left with the community to carry on. Therefore, the seriousness, the continuity, the commitment and the duration of whatever the assistance is should be long-term, durable, so that when the NGO leaves, the community can carry the work on their own. For this reason, it is being constantly advocated that the attitude of such voluntary organisations in assisting communities should be to develop independence in the community members by urging them to participate as owners of the project. Very often communities are hardly trained to realize that assistance is only for a short-time and that eventually the community has to carry on the project work on their own. Therefore, many NGOs just come and go and this makes it difficult to assess their contribution to the project. However, the record of many well-organized and established NGOs show their efficiency and competence in achieving their objectives by involving and motivating the target group and making easier rapport with them (Syed Noman, Ahmed, 1997). Things that distinguish worthwhile NGOs from those who do desultory and indifferent work are the following:

1. A spirit of dedication, in spite of odds;
2. willingness to work, in spite of poor remuneration and long hours;
3. a combination of teamwork and communication;
4. a closeness with the community it serves;
5. flexibility and responsiveness to the exigencies of the situation,
6. close and well-guided monitoring; and
7. A seeking for newer and improved strategies (Khalakdina, Margaret, 1998).

Many of the donors to the NGOs are foreign. They hardly visit the sites, do not know the extent of utilization of funds and the progress of the development of the schemes they provide for. They depend mainly upon annually recorded reviews and evaluations which, like many of the Government schemes, are hardly validated. Further, it must be said that donor agencies from out of India like Oxfam, Care, CRS and other such international philanthropic organisations provide funds to the NGOs for specific projects. However, there is some criticism of aid giving donors. "Most commonly we hear the voices of those who say that aid is insufficient and that it should be increased. Some detractors single out specific types of aid as being inappropriate (food aid, for example, or programme aid, or aid for the development of heavy industries)". Others focus on particular instances in which aid has been used wastefully, or corruptly, or has gone to governments that are not politically popular in the West." (Hancock, Graham, 1989).

In the last analysis, however, in such a large country like India, help is needed not only in one aspect but in several packages of services for the poor. These are in the areas of water, food, clothing, health, education and the learning of skills that are marketable and can sustain the participants. However, many national NGOs are not working consistently or on a large scale. Given the heterogeneous nature of the country, NGO efforts are small and their benefits trickle down to the needy in very small amounts. What is evidenced, however, is that for whatever effort is genuinely put in by some genuine organisations that continue over the years, salutary effects are seen, others fall by the wayside through attritioning in services and the siphoning off of donor funds.

It is argued that focusing on the millennium development goals for the majority using the standards enunciated in the goals is not very realistic. Given the great degree of heterogeneity even among the poor who consist of various groups, such as tribal, rural and urban poor, much of the success of program implementation depends upon the active and vigorous participation of the beneficiaries themselves in utilising the various subsidies and the benefit of many programmes in the various states. However, it is well-known that the effect of governmental subsidies, social programmes in health and education vary from one State to another and from one vulnerable group to another. For example, the dalits although they have access to reservation programmes find it difficult to absorb the benefits fully since they are occupied mainly with work for their self-sustenance that takes most of their time. Accessibility to facilities also is an important factor. The further away the group is from the hub of the bureaucracy that implements services as an agency, the less is the development of the group. Further, NGO agencies need to work in close connectivity with the beneficiaries, who are not equal in their abilities with the NGO agents and, therefore, can be exploited. As said before, commitment is varied among NGOs, the budgeting is poor and delayed from the donors, record-keeping and reporting takes up much of the time and the field agents of NGOs are sometimes themselves not experts in the enterprises they wish to promote. For example, to develop allied agricultural activities like poultry, bee-keeping and even fish-cultivation requires expertise from among the NGO field agents who many times do not have the necessary expertise and so the work is done in a desultory fashion.

In some States, the process by which the institutions raised by the NGOs help poverty reduction is the creation of a savings fund. These saving funds are contributed to by the members in a revolving manner. Some NGOs have adopted the model of the Gramin banks in Bangladesh. These NGOs helped form the support network for the poor to avail of micro-finance from rural banks. Those among the NGOs which did well in supporting community groups were those which had leadership, group knowledge and commitment, and those whose their motives were homogeneous with those of the group/community they work with.

There are of course numerous single-handed volunteers who on their own are doing community work as in the case of the education of street children, the holding of *Mahila* Meetings in urban slums and assisting entrepreneurial activities in arts and crafts, because of their innate enthusiasm and commitment. They are in the main fairly successful because they make participants feel that they own their own enterprises/group of activities. Yet, we still have to ask the question, why is it that the Government does not assist such worthwhile enterprises, expand the work which is genuine and which has some sustainability when people themselves participate in their own programmes.

We know that as of today primary school education is still poorly implemented. Education has been emphasized since the initiation of the Five Year plans and more recently reemphasized with the introduction of the *Right to Education Act*. The rural and tribal people are hardly interested since this type of education is irrelevant to the traditional jobs in which they are occupied.

So, there seems to be a vicious circular action and reaction so long as the implementers do not concentrate on ground level realities. The implementers are content with the reading of reports and reviews which may be and most probably are given in exaggerated figures, and in the conduct of meetings which many times are inconclusive. Even today we are aware of the various programmes righteously implemented, but cut-short by the pocketing of funds by the implementers. We are well-aware of the fact that at the local level some of the programmes implemented are deliberately made "show pieces" so as to appease the visiting dignitary from either the bureaucracy or the polity, but in actual fact after the visitors go away, the programme falls into its usual slow pattern of indifference.

Continuing with this theme of facetiously called "developmental programmes" meant for the poor, we need to distinguish the various ideologies of governance. Governance, generally speaking and in its simplest form, means the political control and management of the facilities and amenities of a group of people living in a common territory or country. The members of the group live according to the rules and regulations of the stated policies of governance. In order that there is a structure and system in which this governance occurs, rules and regulations are put into place to be followed in an ethical manner by all members of the group. Rules and mandates are monitored by the Government leaders, whether elected or in the bureaucracy. Translated into the interactions within the represented people, ideologies form the framework of governance. These ideologies are termed democracy, communism and autocracy. The operational labels are capitalism, socialism, and militarism, respectively. For example, North America's governance is based on capitalism. This means everybody has the privilege of rising to their highest capacities in terms of access to wealth and power. In a democracy, people pay taxes based on the wealth they earn. Wealth can only be acquired in an ethical manner, based on one's own efforts.

Autocracy is based on authoritarianism, where leadership is not shared but rests on one individual's decision-making power or the continuance of the individual's dynasty in a hierarchical manner. This happens where the leader uses his own set of law and order systems. The contribution to the exchequer is decided by the leader/s of the ruling autocracy. In authoritarianism or autocracy, as found in some countries in South America, and in some tribal societies as in some of the countries of Africa, the mandates of the leader cannot be contravened.

Communism is squarely based on the principle of sharing work and wealth equally, so that no one person is economically better off than the other. Communism forms a union of one mind, one people. There is little transgression without punishment and lesser freedom of action and speech than in capitalist countries because the system of law and order was and is to be strictly followed without bias towards any one individual.

These ideologies are not "stand-alone" ideologies. There are different mixtures. In India, we have a form of capitalism-cum-social-welfare *potpourri* of governance system. What is important for India is that its governance is said to be based on the democratic system and, therefore, it follows that the political structure is expected to be systematically representative. It also includes a system of assisting those who are in need of basic services. This it does through subsidies and free services like offering social benefits for those who are termed as weaker sections of the society. Some of the social welfare measures that exist in Western countries like unemployment benefits do not exist in India, except for the newly introduced Employment Guarantee Scheme, as they would be a drain on the Government's exchequer as the numbers to be helped are extremely large and the revenues are inadequate. This is mainly due to the fact that only a small number of people working in government and professional institutions pay taxes while the larger proportion of people do not do so.

In this document we will not go into the details of each ideology except to say that they are liable to change dynamically from time to time as we are currently witnessing in the Middle East countries which were previously under autocratic rulers and are now moving out of their stranglehold and trying to formulate their own ideologies.

In terms of its governance, India is said to be a democracy in that it follows democratic principles in its planning and programming for development and its implementation. Its major theme is empowerment of the target group for it is *by the people, for the people, and of the people*. There are legislatures, both at Central and State levels. These legislative bodies make laws through a system of introduction, reading, discussing and passing of Bills in and by the legislature. Bills can be rejected and re-introduced. Political Parties come into leadership positions on a periodic basis through general elections held every five years. If a major Party falls short of the required numbers to be able to form a government, it co-opts other Parties to form a coalition. This encourages political leaders to keep mushrooming parties so that they can have their own little say at the time of legislation or append themselves to powerful parties so that they can fall under its umbrella.

Unfortunately, those who know more about governance are the people in Parliament, in the Political Parties and the bureaucracy, while the poor are blissfully ignorant of the rights and privileges that should accrue to them and therefore are exploited. Their constituent politicians are least interested in informing them and guiding them to improve their conditions.

Ironically, the curious position in India is that while it has declared itself to be a democracy based on the principle of "Equality for all", in fact equality does not exist for all. The larger proportion of people who are poor are certainly not equal to the smaller powerful wealthy group, who tend to keep themselves at a distance from the poor majority. This in fact is more pronounced given the parameters of the caste system and social class and regional differences. Fraternity is barred by the long-standing socio-religious differences and divisions of castes and Jatis; and, finally, Justice while available is hardly utilized by the poor since they are ignorant of the laws, orders and the binding necessities in order to understand how applicable they are. Even when they do, they do not have the necessary finances to engage lawyers to fight for their rights. Lawyers in their turn know that these poor are so ignorant that it made no difference if they overcharge which they usually do. Therefore, the cases of the poor, if at all come to the courts, languish, get delayed and gradually fall out of the purview of the courts of law and justice.

Many of the poor are so illiterate that all that they can to acquiesce is to affix their thumb impressions to the given documents. They are forcefully made aware of their penalties when transgressing laws in petty matters.

In 2011, the Government of India introduced a National Food Security Bill. This is planned to provide food security to the masses of the poor Indian population. Under this law, 7 kg of food grains per person per month is expected to be given at subsidized rates to a category of "priority households" consisting of not less than 46 per cent of the rural population and 28 per cent of the urban population and not less than 3 kg of food grain per person per month to a category of "general households" under the Targeted Public Distribution System. The total households thus targeted would cover 75 per cent of the rural population and 50 per cent of the urban population. This scheme is a modification of the Public Distribution System which had been in operation for several decades. The latter, however, failed as it was too little for too many and in many cases was sabotaged by the shopkeepers themselves because of their corrupt practices, which included selling of the foodgrains meant for distribution to the poor in the open market (Khera, Reetika, 2011). India has to have a huge continuous stock of food items available for any successful implementation of such an ambitious food distribution programme. Ironically, we hear of tons and tons of staple food lying out in the open and rotting because of the inadequacy of storage facilities, leave alone the management of the huge distribution structure and system that would be required to realize the objectives of the Food Security Bill. The fate of the new plan for food security is likely to fall into the same pitfalls as did the public distribution system because the infrastructure, the personnel and the distribution system are faulty. It is like pouring new wine into old casks and the result would be the same as before.

Overriding these lacunae is the greatest of all, namely, the lack of an ethical, transparent and accountable governance, inspite of the elaborate and high-sounding rhetoric in the Five Year Plan documents, and by the political leadership of the country. In fact, the XI Plan document emphatically stated that "inclusive growth, reducing poverty and bridging the various divides that continue to fragment our society can only be achieved if there is a significant improvement in the governance" which must be "accountable and transparent" especially towards the poor (Government of India, 2007). Inclusiveness specifically implies the inclusion of the greater majority who are still "forgotten"; those who are below the poverty line and those who constitute the largest proportion of the population who are still way behind in productive skills and knowledge of science and technology. Thus, inclusion in development seems to be the sole prerogative of the miniscule elite sections of society.

Historically, whatever the ideology and forms of governance may be, there is an absence of a purely ethically-intentioned regime. This is hidden under the mantle of a seemingly committed polity. At whatever level the governance occurs, whether at the global, the national, the State or the township level, the priority of the polity continues to be self-preservation and self-enhancement. It is said that there is no parliamentarian who is not rich. This may be quite possible considering there are several hundreds who have stashed away their black money in foreign tax-free banks. Lobbying, bestowing favours, and taking "commissions" are some of the expressions of self-centered governance. During elections, in any country, a great deal of benefits are promised. Actions which would raise the ire of the people all subdued till the elections are over as each one is trying to outwit the other in accumulating a large vote-bank and so the vicious cycle continues as before. It is only the mantle that will change. Whichever the Party in power, the same ego-centric approach would tend to prevail. Parties will look after their own interests before those of others: the others implying "the masses out there". This is not to say that these attitudes, values and actions are true of all those in power, but there seems to be a system of "follow the leader", where the top brass is seen to be callous of promises made but not kept. There are still upright people among politicians who continue to abide by the policy and law, and raise their voices for the poor. However, they are so few in number that over a period of time their voices get subdued and forgotten. This situation is similar to the corruption and scam cases which are on a high tone in the initial situation, but then get conveniently pushed under the carpet. This is because, the enormities of those who see their power and positions as a means for serving self-interests soon push the upright people out of their positions, so that the latter are non-threatening to those who have fallen into corrupt ways.

It must be admitted, however, that India is segmented into too many differential divisions with a kind of heterogeneity which defies analysis. This makes it difficult to look at the country in a holistic manner. For example, though the principle of "secularism" is accepted in theory, the religious divisions in society give rise to tensions and confrontations as seen in the *Ayodhya Ram Janam Bhoomi* versus *Babri Masjid* controversy.

As said before, there are also different levels of economic well-being among the States. The richer States have to provide larger amounts to the Federal or Central revenue through a system of intricate taxation. The people in poor States contribute very little to the exchequer as many of them are not permanent employees in either the government or the private sectors and are usually casual workers in agricultural and urban sectors. The people in the poor States resent their levels of poverty and, therefore, indulge in widespread protests, rallies and Satyagrahas, as they experience the humiliation of being poor and neglected. Further, Inter-State tensions increase when facilities are shared. An example of this is the contention between Karnataka and Tamil Nadu over sharing of waters of Godavari river.

Again within each State, there are confrontations between tribals and non-tribals, for often the industrialists belonging to the latter grab the land of the former at meager compensatory rates. There have been, for some time now, persistent demands for separate States in some larger States as a result of which new States have been created like Chhattisgarh, Jharkhand and Uttarakhand. There are continuing agitations for the creation of States like Gorkhaland in north-east Bengal and Telengana in Andhra Pradesh. There has also been advocacy for further division of Uttar Pradesh into four States for ease of administration, whether those who advocate this have hidden motives of gaining political power in the divided parts of this largest State seems to be a moot question. There are also the continuing separatist insurgencies in the State of Jammu & Kashmir and the North East, which are worrying problems for the government.

The very heterogeneity of 28 separate States and 7 Union Territories makes for a Jigsaw puzzle for planning and implementation at the State levels which create problems of coordination at the Central level. This affects the development of the poor who are at the lowest rung of the socio-economic ladder. The destabilization caused by the division, re-division and the infighting affect the status of the poor more than it does the rich. The planning process in India, at whichever level, is so complex and interrelated in an intricate manner that even the very educated find it difficult to quote rules and regulations in order to justify their stance. The Plan allocations to the various States also have a bias towards those States which are run by the members of the ruling Coalition at the Centre. When there are different parties ruling at the state *vis a vis* at the Centre, differences in perception lead to misunderstanding and confrontation. It is not unusual to find that some States overspend their budget and still others have surpluses which they are unable to use because of the lack of infrastructure and personnel to implement them or because of mismanagement or delayed action. What is worse, the Central Government does not have an effective and efficient system to monitor how monies are spent as its monitoring system depends on making of reports, written and counter-written, at the State-level. In a sense, paper work seems to dominate the governance of the country.

The major focus of governance in India in the post-LPG (Liberalisation, Privatisation and Globalisation) period had been to accelerate economic growth in terms of GDP. But, the prerogative of accruing the benefits of the higher GDP seems to have been limited to the unholy alliance of the businessman, the politician and the bureaucrat. The middle class and the poor remained outside the pale of economic growth. The Government, both at the Central and State levels, are unable to stabilize consumer prices which have doubled and trebled over the past decades and hit the poorest the greatest. This has led to the curious anomaly that, at the macro level, India is growing economically even in contrast to some Western countries, while internally it has the largest proportion of the world's poorest. It is those who are business people, industrialists, financiers, property dealers, who are making money, hand over fist. In such a disorganized array of people and their heterogeneity, governance is always in a state of flux, with regard to the well-being of the majority of its people. While the governance ruling through its bureaucracy is in a state of continual adjustment, the private sector seems to be striding well-ahead on its own efforts.

A further factor regarding governance is the changing demographic scenario. As time moves on relentlessly, the elderly grow proportionately in greater numbers than the younger productive generation. According to the Census data, the proportion of the elderly population grew from about 5.6 per cent in 1961 to 7.4 per cent in 2001. According to the Indian Human Development Survey (IHDS) data collected in 2005, the percentage of elderly is said to be even higher at 8 per cent (Sonalde B. Desai, Amaresh Dubey, Brij Lal Joshi, Mitali Sen, Abusaleh Shariff, and Reeve Vanneman, 2010). Consequently, there are now more aged and unproductive Indians, who have to depend upon the household, or the community or the State, and more especially upon their productive young children. The growing dissonance in attitudes and values between the old and the young generations is increasing in view of the effect of globalization and modernisation. This takes its toll on the relationship between the young and the old.

Membership in formal organisations is indicative of the integration of a group of people within geographical parameters. Exclusion, on the other hand, is indicative of fragmented relationships among communities of the various castes where the lower castes, females, poor minorities are less included in formal development activities (Dev Nathan and Virginius Xaxa, 2012).

We may identify five principles which hold communities together in a cohesive manner:

(1) Availability and accessibility of amenities and facilities to all equally.
(2) Little incongruence of different castes, classes and ethnic groups living together in the same residential area.
(3) Availability and accessibility to free and complete school education.
(4) Treatment of females on an equality basis with males.
(5) Easy communication and available infrastructure from one geo-ecological area to another.

The above presents a scenario where there is free and open communication between men and women as to the best situation that assists the total family and the total community.

The governance of health and educational programmes in India leaves much to be desired regarding its quality and effectiveness.

What are the evils that beset the governance in India from attaining a higher quality? The Prime Minster of India in his speech on the 22nd May, 2011 had frankly acknowledged that corruption is hampering the quality of governance. However biased the promises of the ruling party are, the fact remains that they are not in complete control of governance since they have to deal with many coalition partners and a strong opposition. This situation necessitates a great deal of compromises, some of them not in the best interests of the poor, but could reflect an appeasement among the parties.

India's record on the corruption index is very high. Transparency International's Global Corruption Index places India at the 87th position, out of the 178 countries surveyed (Transparency International India, 2010). A number of factors have been cited for the high levels of corruption in India. The lack of accountability on the part of those in power is one of them (Sinha, Pratyush, 2012]. Administrations in India are given extraordinary powers, but they are not held accountable for the results that they are expected to achieve or the delays or losses that they might be directly responsible for (Dr. E. Sreedharan, 2012). This lack of accountability is in turn contributed by dysfunctional administrative system characterized by the lack of an efficient disciplinary process and a well-functioning justice system. One other reason is the absence of incentives for honest, upright decision-making and action.

It was reported that 120 of India's 522 Parliament Members were facing criminal charges as of December 2008 (Peshawania, Rajeev, 2011). This indicates that the roots of corruption are strong. Many Parliamentarians have not yet disclosed their incomes for the purposes of taxation and still others have huge amounts of undeclared assets which are not uncovered, whether by accident or intent.

Thus the corruption of administrators and politicians is understood to be the most debilitating factor in the implementation of programmes for the poor. There is not much connectivity between what is promised and what happens at the ground level in terms of social reality for the poor who are short-changed from their rightful share of the Government's development budget.

There have been various suggestions and demands from people from different walks of life for solving the malady of corruption and non-accountability of politicians and administrators. Some have urged upon the need for creating new political and other institutions that would incentivize good behaviour and honesty (Dr. Jayaprakash Narayan, 2012).

For this reason, there is a persistent demand from the civic society groups in India for instituting a powerful authority, at the Central level (Lokpal) and State level (Lokayuktas) to look into the complaints of corruption of politicians and bureaucrats and to prosecute and recommend punishment for those found to be guilty of such corruption. These are all airy perspective plans.

It is also said that there is a high sounding Bill passed on the Right to Education of the child. This seems to be ironical in the face of the fact that the right to education has existed since the days of the formulation of the Constitution. The fact remains that the situational determinant of poverty forces large numbers of boys and girls at the primary school level to have to drop out of school since their priority is their occupation for their livelihood. How can this situation be altered by just proclamations of Bills, Acts and arduous debates and discussions which take up the time of

Parliamentary speech-making with little action transferred to the ground level? Such situations occur with many other such Acts that have been passed by the Indian Parliament, but are languishing for poor implementation. For example, women are still harassed against inspite of the fact that there is an Act against domestic violence. This Act is still flouted as there is little monitoring of its implementation and there is still no evaluation of the impact of this Act. The same goes for the Dowry Prohibition Act, and such like. At the Central Parliament level, the Act allowing one-third of the seats in the Parliament for women is still dragging its feet. This is understandable since it is well-known that the Indian society is mainly patriarchal and is reluctant to give equal opportunities to women.

Thus, the factor of wealth and its power is most obvious in the way it is manoeuvered by the rich, in the management development of the poor which is more factually the mismanagement of the development of the poor.

To obtain adequate voters to represent the poor requires a great deal of art in the craftiness of advertising one's ideal and supposedly ethical promises. The cash for vote system is long known, but has not been probed for its corruptibility, except just recently. It is jokingly said that if certain politician comes into power he will ensure that there will be a five-star hotel in Tihar jail because of the probability that he and his compatriots will have to be in jail some time or the other.

There is a great deal of money being spent on electioneering campaigns beyond the stipulated amount, but nobody questions this over-expenditure or its source. Where does this extra money come from? Logically, it is from undeclared wealth.

Hierarchical lineage and autocracy can continue *ad infinitum*. Therefore, the Party that is voted to power for a period of time has to prove its value in meeting its stated goals and its progress or regress. This is measured by polls which are carried out from time to time. Again, we must state that not all bureaucrats are corrupt. But, an upright bureaucrat often comes into conflict with the corrupt, but the matters get quickly hushed up by either finding a reason to demote the upright person or to transfer him. What we are saying here is that the voice of the upright bureaucrat and perhaps even an upright politician here and there is stifled by the corrupt.

REFERENCES

Alam, Javed, 2010, "Is Caste Appeal Casteism?", in S. Jodhka, *Community and Identities: Contemporary Discourses on Culture and Politics in India.* Sage Publication, New Delhi: pp. 97-110.

Alok Misra, 2006, *Micro Finance in India and Millennium Development Goals: Maximising Impact on Poverty*. Discussion paper for Workshop on World Bank, Singapore, 18th September 2006.

Anand Kumar, 2003, "Political Sociology of Poverty In India: Between Politics of Poverty and Poverty of Politics", CPRC-IIPA Working Paper No. 3, Chronic Poverty Research Centre (CPRC), Manchester, UK, published as a Chapter in Aasha Kapur Mehta, Sourabh Ghosh, Deepa Chatterjee, Nikhila Menon (eds.), *Chronic Poverty in India,* IIPA/CPRC, 2003;

Copestake, James G., 1996, "The resilience of IRDP: Reform and Perpetuation of An Indian myth", *Development Policy Review,* 14, 51-68.

Carstairs, G.M., 1957, *The Twice Born: A Study of the Community of High Caste Hindu*. London: Hogath.

Craig Johnson, 2003, *Decentralisation in India: Poverty, Politics and Panchayati Raj,* London: Overseas Development Institute.

Davaer, B.D., 1995, "Gender politics and Mental Health Care", *Economic and Political Weekly,* 30 (45), 2879-86

Deaton, Angus & Alessandro Tarozzi, 2000, "Prices and Poverty in India", Working Papers, 213, Princeton University, Woodrow Wilson School of Public and International Affairs, Research Programme in Development Studies.

Dev Nathan and Virginius Xaxa, 2012, *Social Exclusion and Adverse Inclusion: Development and Deprivation of Adivasis in India,* Delhi: OUP India.

"Decentralization in India: Poverty, Politics and *Panchayati Raj*" (Overseas Development Institute, London, February, 2003.

Dhanagare D.N., 1983, *Peasant Movements in India,* 1920-1950. New Delhi: Oxford University Press.

Dreza, Jean, (2011), "Food Bill Must Have Strong Safeguards for Cash Transfer", *Indian Express* (October).

Government of India, 2007, *Eleventh Five Year Plan (2007-2010) Volume-I Inclusive Growth*. New Delhi. p. 256.

Hancock, Graham, 1989. Lords of Poverty: The Power, Prestige and Corruption in International Aid Business. New York: Atlantic Monthly Press.

Jha, R., 2000, "Reducing Poverty and Inequality in India: Has Liberalisation Helped?" Research Paper, 204, World Institute for

Development Economic Research.

Khan, H. Iltija, 1967, "Consequences of Democratic Decentralization In India," Canadian Public Administration, Volume 10, Issue 2, pages 181–196, June 1967

Khera, Reetika, 2011, "India's Public Distribution System: Utilisation and Impact", *Journal of Development Studies*, 1-23, 07 March.

Kumar, Kundan; Pranab Ranjan Choudhary; Soumendra Sarangi, Pradeep Mishra, Sricharan Behera, 2005, *A Socio-Economic and Legal Study of Scheduled Tribes' Land in Orissa*. Bhubaneswar. Supported by World Bank Unpublished.

Khalakdina Margaret, (1998), "Early Child Care and Education in India: A Perspective", in Mina Swaminathan (ed.), *the First Five Years: A Critical Perspective on Early Childhood Care and Education in India*. pp. 163-194. Sage Publications, New Delhi.

Mahajan, Vijay, and Bharti Gupta Ramola, 1996, "Financial Services for the Rural Poor and Women in India: Access and Sustainability", *Journal of International Development*, 8, No. 2: 211–24

N.C. Saxena, "Current Poverty Alleviation Schemes - A Quick Assessment", Chapter 3 in N. C. Saxena, *Policy and Legal Reforms for the Poor in India*. New Delhi: UNDP.

Narayan, Dr. Jayaprakash, 2012, "Values versus Institutions", in E. Sreedharan and Bharat Wakhlu (eds.), *Restoring Values: Keys to Integrity, Ethical Behaviour and Good Governance*. Delhi, Sage Publications, pp. 73-82

Naveen K Shetty, 2008, *The Microfinance Promise in Financial Inclusion and Welfare of the Poor: Evidence from Karnataka, India*, Working Paper No. 205, ISEC Bangalore, Pages 34.

Osmani, S. R., 1990, 'Social Security in South Asia", in Ahmad, S.E., Dreze, J.P, Hills, J., and Sen A K (Eds), *Social Security in Developing Countries*. Oxford: Clarendon.

Patibandla Srikant, 2009, Tribal Movement in Orissa: A Struggle against Modernisation? Working Paper, No. 215, ISEC, pages 16.

Peshawania, Rajeev, 2011, "Leadership Lessons from the Indian Summer", http:///www.forbes.com accessed on 13/1/2013.

Raghav Gaiha, P. D. Kaushik and Vani Kulkarni, 1998, "Jawahar Rozgar Yojna, Panchayats, and the Rural Poor in India", *Asian Survey*, Vol. 38, No. 10, pp. 928-949.

Rajashekhar, D. 2004, *Micro-Finance and Poverty Alleviation Issues Relating to NGO Programmes in South India*, Working Paper No.146, ISEC, Bangalore.

Sadhna, Arya & Roy Anupama, 2006, *Poverty, Gender and Migration*. New Delhi: Sage publications.

Sankaran, Kamala; Shalini Sinha and Roopa Madhav, 2012 *WIEGO Law*

Pilot Project on the Informal Economy: Forests Background Note"

Sinha, Pratyush, "National Values and Goal of Administration", in E. Sreedharan and Bharat Wakhlu (eds.), 2012, *Restoring Values: Keys to Integrity, Ethical Behaviour and Good Governance*. Delhi, Sage Publications. pp. 149-161.

Sonalde B. Desai, Amaresh Dubey, Brij Lal Joshi, Mitali Sen, Abusaleh Shariff, and Reeve Vanneman (eds.), 2010, Human Development in India: Challenges for a Society in Transition, New Delhi: Oxford University Press, page 139.

Sreedharan, Dr. E. 2012, "Public Administration in India: Facing an Ethical Crisis", in E. Sreedharan and Bharat Wakhlu (eds.), *Restoring Values: Keys to Integrity, Ethical Behaviour and Good Governance*. Delhi, Sage Publications, pp. pp. 57-62.

Sujata, Patel, 2001, "Community, Identity and Politics: The Baliapal Movement', in Jodhkar, S. S. (ed.), *Community and Identities: Contemporary Discourses on Culture and Politics in India*. 140-160. New Delhi: Sage Publications.

Syed Noman, Ahmed, 1997, *Rapid Rural Transformation through Voluntary Action*. New Delhi, MD Publications Private Ltd.

Transparency International India, October 26, 2010, "Corruption Perception Index – 2010: India – Continues to be Corrupt", Press Release at www.transparencyindia.org.

6

The Disjointedness between Stated Plans and their Implementation affecting the Poor

Ever since the country has embarked upon the system of Five Year Plans, and at this point we are now in the XII Five Year Plan period, the efforts of the government to improve the status of the poor have been beset by the "mismanagement" of the implementation of the plans. The underlying cause for this is the corruption that has crept into the developmental strategies at different levels and this is perpetuated by the nexus of the corporate world, the political world and the bureaucratic world. These go hand in hand to stymie the progress of the developmental Plans. The various scams that are increasing in an exponential fashion are not only alarming but also reveal a lack of ethical standards among the people in political and administrative power. It degrades the level of integrity of the governance in the eyes of the other countries of the world.

Although the country is said to be self-sufficient in staple foods, a large proportion of people do not have access to adequate food and other basic necessities for living. The continual rise in prices of food and other essential items of consumption is often way above the capacity of the poor, who form, even by the Governmental estimate of the "people below the poverty line", more than a quarter of the total population (Sonalde B. Desai, Dubey Amaresh, Joshi B.L., Sen Mitali, Sheriff Abusaleh and Vanneman Reeve, 2010). The poor are being pushed to search for more than one job at a time in order to meet the basic necessities for everyday survival. It stands to reason that they can take up jobs only if they happen to be available and if they have the necessary skills for them. Neither of these is existent at an acceptable level.

Those who are farmers continue to suffer due to the vagaries of the monsoon with little substitute for energy or for water supply. It is perhaps easier to find jobs in cities because of the variety of the nature of unskilled jobs. However, moving from agriculture to uncertain urban unskilled jobs depletes farm labour and, therefore, the amount of productivity. The consequence is that almost imperceptibly urban slums are springing up or existing slums are expanding without even the basic necessities.

It is well-known that "poverty alleviation" programmes begin with a huge fanfare but peter out within a short time into some kind of a meaningless programme of no consequence for the welfare and development of the targeted people. What is more concerning is that even such name-sake poverty alleviation programmes are not sustained on a regular basis.

There is also a lack of health insurance for the poor, especially for the fragile sections of the population. India alone has 22 per cent of the world's maternal mortality (UNICEF, 2009). According to an estimate, India's maternal mortality ratio stood at 254 per 100,000 live births in 2008. While the IMR and MMR rates have been further reduced to some extent, they are still concerning in absolute numbers. The Government of India's Health and Family Welfare Ministry concedes that 17 lakh children under five years die annually (Express News Service, "3 per cent dip in infant mortality rate", Indian Express, 30.12.2011). This fall in mortality rates is contributed to by the better developing States like Kerala, Gujarat and Punjab. Most of the other States live on the bounty of nature and the handouts by the government. In these latter States, most of the subsidies given to the poor are mostly eaten up by the various levels of middlemen before it reaches the targeted group.

The review of the Millennium Development goals has revealed that, most economies even in the developed world are short of funds to realize these goals given the current global recession. There are problems within problems in the allocation, planning, and disbursement of funds, like the lopsided priorities as in the case of the disproportionately huge allocations for the military and inadequate allocations for education and health. In a discussion on budget allocations, held by Doordarshan, in the first week of October, 2010 the debate centered on the allocations to military, health and education and such other sectors. It was said that a large amount of the budget was set aside for the procurement of new types of military equipments for warfare. The apportioning of the budget to so called security, both internal and at the borders, is at least 10 times more than that allocated for education, health and welfare. Admittedly, there must be adequate security, and therefore spending for infrastructure, equipments and skilled personnel for these purposes is essential. But the malady is that in the name of development of military capabilities, it is the middlemen who lobby for industrialists and the corrupt politicians and bureaucrats who profit the most. Of course, it must be said that, all countries have lobbyists, especially working for industrialists and business people, who have to look after their own interests in productivity and profit. Therefore, they employ lobbyists for their own industries or undertakings. But, there are very few who lobby for the health and education of the poor. It is being rightly said that there must be a balanced proportion and prioritizing in terms of financial expenditure for the various sectors, and strictly monitored by non-biased ethical leadership.

However, India does not follow a strictly federal system like in the USA. There are certain contours of social welfare democracy since it has such a sizeable proportion of poor in contrast to other countries. So it while carrying on with the system of Parliamentary democracy, it is modified to the extent of its revenue being capable of covering most of the population. The word democracy ultimately means that everybody has a fair chance. The poor in India do not. For the poor people, the word "democracy' is a high-sounding word, for, they do not even know the alphabets of the language, leave alone what this system means.

There is also a systemic error constantly occurring in the implementation of plans related to debt financing, whether at the Central level or at the State level. In fact, it is well-known that many developed counties like America, Germany, the UK and France have large debts and are financing their programmes on borrowed money and interestingly many of them borrow from the erstwhile "communist" countries like China and Russia. The question really is, has the principle of capitalism in the democratic ideology failed? Most of the developed countries live in a debt-ridden status, printing paper money and thus adding to thousands and trillions of dollars in debt. The revenue is often below the required amount, distributed through banking systems which are not regulated so that when they fall, the Government bails them out, thus increasing the total debt. For example, the USA has a debt that runs into double digit trillion dollars. It is well-known that the average American is not accustomed to investing in shares and bonds and credit is the main system by which they can borrow from the future, like living in houses which are mortgaged or on insurance to pay their health bills. When they fail to pay the premium or the mortgage over a period of certain number of months, the bank calls for a foreclosure since the borrower of the property is unable to pay and often mortgaged houses are abandoned because of this inability. Some of these houses do not have much resale value and therefore are bulldozed. These countries are now in turmoil because of lack of appreciation of investments for the future as in Spain and Greece. On the other hand, India does not use paper money as much in exchange for goods, nor does it invest in bonds and shares since the poor do not have money for this kind of investment. India does not spew out money to bail or set on sale its banking system since about half of them are state-owned and registered and therefore have the back-up of the central revenue system. Besides, the poor do not invest in owning property nor do they know what it is to mortgage or to pay in installments. Because of these reasons, the Government has introduced certain palliative measures for the poor like free education and health, subsidies for agriculture and incentives for small-scale entrepreneurs. It has even gone to the extent of offering partially free education and privileges for employment for those in the poor who are Scheduled Castes or Scheduled Tribes and Other Backward Classes.

Further, India has a long tradition of investment in family gold. Until recently, most Indians did not use the banking system, and although gold is not invested in debentures so as to accrue interest, they remain as securities in families to be utilized when direly needed. The fact that the price of gold has increased by leaps and bounds is now creating the phenomenon of the middle class becoming interested in shares, equities and mutual funds so as to obtain profits by investing part of their gold. The poor, on the other hand, are blissfully unaware of these credit and investments systems since in any case they do not possess any worthwhile amount of gold. Unfortunately, the Indian tradition is such that it is a must that more money is spent on marriages and religious ceremonies even though the poor are at a greater debt to the money-lenders for these purposes.

In developed countries, it is not unusual for people to live in houses that are not their own, to drive in cars that are not their own, or even to buy equipments on credit system. Perhaps, it is this insurance against erratic inconsistency in the economy that has made the middle-class Indian investment-minded, especially with the rise in gold prices. This investment has helped raise revenues which have contributed to the growing GDP. While India still has countless unemployed, and their actual percentage is unfathomable, we do know that countries in the west have 8-10 per cent of unemployment rates wobbling their countries, and many of these countries had to bail out their banks through "stimulus packages". India does not fall into this category. The upper and middle class are doing pretty well because of their gold investments. The poor have none and so they stay where they are economically.

Despite India's growing GDP, its expenditure and accountability is still not transparently known. It does not need an analytical mind to know that this growing GDP is not being spent on the poor. It is obvious in the rich and the growing middle classes. The general need for better infrastructure and better systems of management are still relatively poor. Instead, India is going in for large transactions with other countries and so it is becoming more "market-oriented" than "poor-oriented".

The utilization of the GDP is relatively unknown inspite of the rhetoric on it by the governance.

In the days of the old, from the feudal times, Village *Panchayats* were small cohesive groups and there was a system that was followed in settling disputes and maintaining and enforcing customary laws and social practices. Now with the introduction of an official system from the States through the districts to the Block and finally to the Village level, there is little information as to how the funds for the district, block and village level are being utilised or accounted for and relayed back to the top level so that it is known clearly as to whether the expenditure was done for the purpose for which it was meant, namely, development.

However, with the present day commercialization, globalization and the sudden awareness of the outer world, the office-bearers in the *Panchayats* are bewildered by new edicts and are tempted to seek higher commissions in the growing transactions over land and property. Many of the *Pradhans* belong to the upper castes. They soon learn to swipe away the cream of the top of the milk in connivance with the official line of administration.

India is a country of great talkers, speech-makers, promise-givers. This can be bountifully experienced at the time of elections, whether at the Central or State level. Eventually, what is promised to the poor, from whom the politician wrests their votes, is soon forgotten as soon as they are elected. In this scenario, the issue still continues to be "who will speak on behalf of the poor". This is still unknown as there is no systematic effort to back up the rights of the poor except now and again the lone voice of a group of civic society or committed NGOs. Inspite of the many rights, which are still in the form of Bills have yet to be passed for implementation, the situation of developmental programmes, is stymied on most fronts. It is in contrast, mainly to the private sector that is making huge and successful strides ahead of the governmental elephant-like delayed implementations of developmental programmes.

Governmental programmes, in many cases, are not widely spread as there are shortfalls in infrastructures. Before a programme can be implemented, it is essential that the infrastructure and trained personnel are in place. Any project has also to be piloted before being implemented. To this day, there are schools in villages and tribal areas where children sit on the verandahs of their class rooms since the classroom walls are caving in, and both teachers and children are not enthused to appear consistently to teach and learn creatively. There are also programmes related to women like the Development of Women and Children in Rural Areas (DWCRA) and several other programmes of social welfare dotted here and there over the country which over time shrivel up and attrition out of sight. Part of the problem is that every time the Party that comes into power in leading a Government wishes to display its prowess by discarding programmes of previous regimes and conceiving new programmes hastily put together with eye-catching titles so that the public is impressed with the new Party's agenda. Often, the actions do not reflect the words, and the programmes/projects which are initiated with a lot of fanfare by politicians and bureaucrats wither away. There have been many high-sounding words like "people's participation", "community participation", and "community rehabilitation", which in reality have not created permanent inroads and which are insufficiently viable to be continued. The crux of the matter really is the commitment of everybody to everybody else in the programme system, and its implementation where there is still the air of charity-giving from the Government towards the poor.

While the socio-economic class system exists in most countries, India is perhaps the only country which still has the discriminating caste-based system. Caste-barriers and discriminatory socio-religious practices are still rampant in most parts of India. Caste consciousness of some being pure and some being impure seem to overpower the weak adherence to secular constitutional principles enshrined in the Constitution of India, namely, the principles of Equality, Justice, Liberty and Fraternity. This is being exemplified by the fact in schools in many parts of India, the Mid-Day Meal programmes are eschewed by the parents of the upper caste children simply because they have to sit side by side with their lower caste peers during the mid-day meal. Until the Indians themselves realize the debasing nature of this system of caste discrimination, the principles in the Constitution will continue to have less meaning. Further, unless there is a complete change in the situation, where everybody has equal opportunities to compete with everybody else with a level-playing field, just like an Olympic race, where caste does not matter inequality and impoverishment will continue.

India's economy is said to be growing rapidly, with real gross domestic product expanding at an average annual rate in excess of 9 per cent in 2007–2008 and yet amazingly, as of 2010, more than 25 per cent of India's population of 1.35 billion still live below the poverty line. ("Poverty in India" reported at http://www.economywatch.com/indianeconomy/poverty-in-india.html). This is a contradiction in itself, especially from the point of view of those living below the poverty line. It is well-known that tonnes of wheat are lying in the open for want of structure for storage and systems of speedy distribution (news in Times X channel on Television on 9. 5. 2010). Therefore, for academicians, politicians and intellectuals debating on the poverty line with such earnestness and with such variation would be unnecessary if the governance had concentrated on two factors: (1) storage of staples and (2) quick distribution at low prices to the poor. It has been suggested that since every village has a *Panchayhat Ghar*, instead of its being used for periodical political machinations, they may be used for storage of precious grain.

There is wide disparity prevalent in health outcomes between the high-income, high-caste groups and the low-income, low caste groups. Growing inequities, combined with shortages in the provision of primary health care and the rising cost of health care, are complicating the country's efforts to meet the health and nutrition related Millennium Development Goals. It is well-known that in the various primary health centers and state-run hospitals meant for the poor, the services are grossly inadequate. We have often heard that villagers who trek miles to health centers find to their chagrin either the personnel are not there, or the medicines are "out of stock". In fact, it is well-known that the doctors who are given duties in these primary health centers and hospitals are busy in their own private practice, and the medicines meant for supplying to the poor are sold in the black-market without any guilt or conscience.

It seems that there is a heavy concentration on economic growth without giving adequate attention to the social well-being and human resource development. Making money is of little use if it is not primarily used for the health and welfare of the people themselves, and such is the case with the poor and the neglected. If the country has a large proportion of healthy people, the tendency would be for them to be energetic to seize opportunities to be skillful and therefore turn around the profile of the economy of the country. The UN meeting in September, 2010 to assess the progress of the Millennium Development Goals has come to the conclusion that progress is not only slow but that the gap between the needs of meeting the Poor's basic facilities and their funding has regressed as population has increased in these developing countries.

Those who become rich and those who suddenly acquired wealth tend to spend on conspicuous consumption rather than on health, hygiene and better education. Ironically, the poor have not had a chance to experiment with sudden riches. Unfortunately, people from other countries when they talk about India, while they are admirers of its culture and heritage, often say that it is a country of three 'D's, namely, Dirt, Disease and Decay.

Development aid to India is crucial. However, now that recession has set in, other countries are keen to sell their armaments and military technology to India which is more useful to them considering that these countries borrow in millions from other well-to-do countries in the far-east like China. In the name of development, the money given by donors is utilized on consultants, for equipments which is not really well-used, for holding of seminars and conferences and very negligently utilized for the well-being of the poor for whom the donor aid was meant to be spent (Masud, Nadai & Yontcheva, Boariana, 2005).

Technology, while exhibiting its prolific rise in the country, has also been brought to the notice of the poor through social media. The poor have also been attracted to the buying of cellular phones which is a juxtaposition in view of their poverty. These electronic gadgets do not really serve the purpose of their physical and social well-being and instead is merely a display of technological acquisition. In fact, many of those who belong to the lower classes keenly display their acquisition of mobiles which they can ill-afford but still they continue to use them for social talk.

These modern technological equipments only create a sense of frustration amongst the poor who cannot afford them. However, the existence of the modern world of technology and the world of the poor which again represents power and powerlessness respectively, are in an uneasy co-existence. The poor who work as domestic servants in the houses of the rich, are exposed to their wealth and yet when they are back home they are living a life of drudgery and hardship, which is in sharp contrast to the life of the elite and creates a sense of frustration.

The temptation is so great that the frustrated poor, especially the youth, have either to acquire earning skills faster to enable them to avail of these gadgetry or be so frustrated that they resort to illegal means of acquisition like stealing, cheating and other petty crimes. This is a matter of concern because imperceptibly the youth in the poor sections are growing in greater numbers than in the miniscule upper classes. This means that unconsciously, we are building up a great wave of frustration among the youth and possible confrontation of them with those who have and with those who represent them in the polity, the bureaucracy and the business world.

The young generation is, therefore, beset with problems, such as lack of quality education, lack of well-paid jobs and the perception of sophisticated living which is out of their reach. This is the future generation and if this future generation is contributed to by the millions of poor, less educated, poorly skilled youth, one can imagine that what the future generation in terms of the societal impact would be like.

Foreign aid which comes in the form of development projects, for instance, in the medical area, indicates that more doctors, especially in the health centers for the poorer sections of society, are acting as interpreters for foreign donors and as desk writers for reporting back and forth, rather than utilizing their skills for their practice. If nothing else, the medical professionals pay more attention to their private practice which is lucrative and less attention is given to their scheduled work in rural and tribal areas and urban slums. Therefore, we come to the conclusion that even while the country is rich with items of conspicuous consumption, the poor are left by the way side to fend for themselves with the rising prices even of the staple food and other essential items of consumption. Thereby, this might lead to less healthy condition and greater stress.

At the same time, the poor see before their very own eyes how the rich get richer by corrupt practices and, therefore, try to imitate these corrupt practices. To them, such corrupt practices seem to be the only way of being able to afford a better standard of living. In this, however, the poor are at a discount, as they have neither the skills nor the opportunity. The only option left with them is to imitate the corrupt ways in their own little spheres, like taking bribes for petty jobs, committing petty crimes and resorting to treachery and robbery. So, one might say that developmental aid and a great GDP has a distressing effect on the poorer sections of people, especially the young.

This disjointedness between the proclaimed policy ethics and the reality at the ground level can only portend a social ethic that is not in congruence with the economic ethics. National proclamations are, therefore, not local realities. It has been suggested that perhaps local governance would diminish the occurrence of "policy paralysis" as to its strategies.

Traditionality and Modernity

The average Indian in the heterogeneous population in various States and belonging to various castes, classes and ethnicities has nevertheless a core of homogeneous values which are socio-religious in nature in which fortunately he finds his roots of identity. These socio-religious values emanate from religious injunctions of the Hindu scriptures which is the dominant religion in India. These values pervade the whole socialisation process, but yet being exposed during the adolescent years to the world of modernisation, the average Indian tends to imitate the model he or she perceives. Further, modernisation brings with it a tendency to accumulate wealth even at the expense of hazardous disadvantages. This is illustrated by the recent incident of a calamity which occurred in an upper class hospital in Kolkata, West Bengal, where due to the negligence, greed and lack of ethics of the hospital authorities in storing highly inflammable materials in the basement of the hospital, a devastating fire broke out and many of the patients died of suffocation. The post-facto enquiries revealed that, the authorities responsible for inspecting and monitoring did not comply with the rules and regulations regarding safety and therefore stored the basement with inflammable materials. This implies a lack of commitment on the part of those responsible for the health of its people. Responsible public officials, from an ordinary policeman to a Police Inspector to a Registrar, who are supposed to check wrong-doings, wilfully neglect to do so. The wrong-doings are forgiven or are overlooked for the exchange of commissions. There can be numerous illustrations from the everyday experiences of the common man where the latter are taken for granted, indicating a loosening hold on ethical conduct.

This is also observable in the upper elite who are absorbing modernizing patterns of behaviour over and beyond the westernized mode. Time is resilient with changes in patterns of behaviour as influenced by national and global events. There is a strong tendency in the Indian populace to imitate the patterns of behaviour of the west brought to them by social media and globalization. These changes occur at various rates among the different socio-economic groups. In the urban areas, nowadays, almost everyone has a mobile. They are familiar with metros and are conversant with newspapers/television. Therefore, there is a dynamic interchange of behaviour between traditional and modernized modes dependent upon influencing situations. But uniquely in India both patterns exist side by side and the average Indian can instantaneously change from one mode to the other, living a dual pattern best illustrated by child-labourers in market places who have ragged clothes, but are talking into mobiles. In the upper classes, young executives go partying to pubs over the weekend and there are loose heterosexual activities during leisure time.

These changes are initiated by the younger informed generation whereas the older generations tend to hold on to age-old traditional patterns. Irrespective of the mandates of democratic India, the depth of its meaning has yet to be absorbed by the average Indian who represents almost the 70 percent of the population living in dire circumstances.

These patterns are observable where there is a juxtaposition between modernity and traditionality in almost all cities.

However, there is a wide gap between the people of the metropolises and the hinterland. What the poor have as entertainment is perhaps listening to songs and *bhajans* and watching the rare *Nautanki* actors when they go around villages and perhaps listen to music over the public address system when there is a marriage or a feast. Some of them by sheer luck, if they live in places where there is electricity might have a TV and that is all. Therefore they are far-removed from the imitation of modern ways. As such the youth in the rural areas are only attuned to what their environment gives them which is often bleak and routine. Those who break-away and go to urban areas even if there as a lack of hygiene, health and education prefer to stay on since they want to emulate the ways of the rich. If the rural areas had some form of entertainment, better education facilities and were taught better lifestyles in health and hygiene, perhaps they would have continued to stay in their places of origin rather than move as unknown people into urban slums.

The debilitating conditions of the poor are not significantly addressed by the rulers, namely, the politicians. The poor are pacified by words like *"hah, ho jayenga* (yes, it will happen), *thodi* se *der* (a little while longer), *haanji aaj ho jayega* (will happen today) and such like palliative empty words, to appease the larger poor masses. However an up and coming new phenomenon is the burgeoning middle class. Imperceptibly, they are becoming more aware of their rights and privileges and much of the upheaval about the prevalent scams are being brought to the surface by enquiries through the social media and using the privilege of the Right to Information Act introduced in 2009. These are new avenues available to the middle class for knowing about their rights and privileges. It is of course logical to assume that the burgeoning of the middle class is due mainly to their becoming educated, professional and need-oriented to raise their status of living. This middle class is becoming more aware of such phenomena as cash for votes, tax havens, giving commissions and slicing of money meant for development programmes. This awareness is evident in the awakening of the civic society who protest for the rights of the average man (*aam admi*). Essential services for the most needy, for contributing to a sense of well-being, are sparse, especially for those living in inaccessible areas. The polity is keenly aware of such lacuna, but if at all they help, it is only for those in their own constituencies and only in a palliative way, using delaying tactics and other means of putting off the actual delivery of services.

The business world is keen on acquisition of the lands of poor for mere pittances and even the business executive is busy with assisting the business man and the politician in their own interested areas, as they also enjoy the privilege of "being commissioned".

Therefore, the situation remains more or less the same, if not increasing, whatever party is in power. It is only if the burgeoning middle class is knowledgeable and makes efforts to bring to light irregularities in governance, corruptions and scams that some steps might be taken for initiating ethical conduct in the governance system.

Justice itself is under scrutiny and there have been cases of impropriety in the meting out justice. It is those who are aware of the injunctions of the law who can learn means of using strategies to evade taxation. The poor usually do not have permanent jobs which pay pensions and, therefore, have to live on what little they earn whenever they earn. They are either agricultural labourers, other labourers in rural areas or daily-wage earners in urban areas. So, on two counts the facilities for the poor are lacking. The first is the evasion of taxes by those who are knowledgeable about ways and means of evading them, and the second is, the no tax liability for the large majority of the poor because of their non laxible income. This leads to paucity in government revenues to provide adequate infrastructure and basic facilities for the poor and yet in this process skimming away of the benefits to the target group continues.

It is well-known by now that materials and their management poorly implemented lead to poor output. As regards the poor, very few of the top officials are interested in quality or output, nor are they consistent about management and its implementation. The major outcomes of their programmes are what interest the polity. The truth of the matter is that work in rural areas is poorly paid and desultory. Therefore, there is often a preference for better-paying jobs in urban areas however erratic. The poor also prefer urban areas because of the better availability of amenities.

Programmes meant for them are poorly planned and managed. The upper castes who already have kickstart in schools, usually accrue to themselves the best jobs and the better grades which then lowers the self-esteem of the less better off trying to compete with the former. It is well-known that admissions to prestigious educational institutions are also preceded by "capitation fees," donations which the poor cannot afford. Those who can afford such donation get their children admitted to such prestigious educational institutions irrespective of whether their children are meritorious or not. Also, merit students are often frustrated by the fact that they are displaced by the seats reserved for Scheduled Castes, Scheduled Tribes and Other Backward Classes. There are often instances where such meritorious children belonging to the upper castes resort to obtaining by bribery failure certificates indicating that they belong to the Scheduled Castes or Scheduled Tribes in order to gain admission. This issue is beset with problems which should be looked at in a new frame by the governance. Instead, if proper attention is paid to the lower caste children right from the inception from the primary school with attractive incentives, then the likelihood is that they may bloom in their potentials and become just as meritorious as the upper caste children. However, it is well-known that children from the lower castes cannot spare the time even to finish their primary school. They are, therefore, short-changed in the development of their potentials and skills.

The above instances are given to illustrate the fact that the written codes in these government laws are incomprehensive to the poor who are mainly illiterate and, therefore, cannot take advantage of privileges and continue to go along the lines that they have traditionally been accustomed to. Otherwise, they believe in the promises made to them by their constituent politicians. The poor feel that the bond of patronage is still prevalent in the patron's relationship with them, but it is well-known that once the politician has been elected the latter go their own way.

Further, the adherence to civic laws is somewhat dubious with the average Indian. Petty rules are often transgressed if there is no supervision. For example, an individual will cross the road even when the red light is on. Again, the person in a hurry to travel by train will do so without reservation and when the ticket collector comes around he will try to bribe him to allow him to continue his journey. There are several such illustrations where unscrupulousness is practised when there is low overseeing of adherence to the law. These transgressors of the law do not know the fine nuances of the law and, even if they are right, they do not know how to petition for reprieve and succumb to their convoluted interpretation of justice.

The term freedom is less understood since in its abstract form the laws regulating this freedom towards ethical behaviour is unknown to the unlettered poor. In actual fact, the word "freedom" is not translatable to the poor because the poor are bound by their own poor circumstances which compel them to lead a harsh life of survival with little time to understand the significance of such high-sounding terminology. There is no freedom in violating rules. But, there is freedom in giving bribes. There is no freedom in being victims of the rich. But there is freedom in serving the rich. Even to this day, a bureaucrat is called "*Sahib*", or "Sir", by those who are below his status. It is something ingrained in the nature of the Indian who tends to behave in an abnegative manner.

The average Indian does not know that freedom implies acting on the basis of certain civic laws and regulations and they interpret them to suit their conveniences. Further, the average Indian is unaware of what access to freedom means because he only understands its converse interpretation that is, he is not free to do "as he likes." Fraternity implies brotherhood. This term is used only in the formulations of formal political declarations like "*hum log sab bhai, bhai hain*" (We are all brothers). This principle should literally mean, we all have access to freedom irrespective of caste, class, religion, ethnicity or sex. Being a patriarchal country, the use of the male gender term "bhai" is used for anybody irrespective of the status, not because they incorporate the real biological meaning but is mainly used as interjection in conversation, such as *"arey, bhai, aapko samaj mei nahi aa a hai"* (Oh, brother, you don't understand what it is) We frequently hear which housemistresses call their working servant *"beta"*, where there is no real meaning of bondage, but is just an expression to get the work done. In this way, the poor are being cheated of their rightful status when they hear these binding terms. However, not to be outdone, they in turn use expressions like "anty ji", "mata ji", to the strange female in shops and elsewhere when they have to address them.

Even to this day, the female sex is denigrated and has to depend upon the Feminist Movement to plead the right to be a citizen irrespective of gender. This is because from time immemorial, the female has always been the "second sex", with respect to rights and privileges and we assume that this continues to be so in the face of the stranglehold of the patriarchal system.

The word "liberty" has only a nominal meaning. It does not imply liberty to do what one likes, but it really means that there is freedom to talk without feeling constrained in what one likes to say or do. There are strictures, injunctions and various restrictions so that law and order might be maintained and one is not at liberty to do as one likes. This term is less understood by the poor while the educated rich and high-powered status people know how to manipulate these terms when dealing with the poor who are uneducated and naïve. The latter might have liberty within the four walls of their residence, but beyond that the laws of citizenry keep them in check.

We see, therefore, that even for those who have some smattering of education, the far reaching implications of such laws, injunctions, principles and statutory mandates, are accepted as generalizations of an ideology, but in operational terms little understood by the poor.

The above description of the current state of social and economic well-being or otherwise in the country is born out by the facts of the five year plan assessments. Sixty years after Independence and the high-sounding implications of the

Constitutional Directives, many developmental programmes for the poor are poorly implemented.

By now the reader is well-aware of the unique social and economic differences between the miniscule rich and the large masses of the poor. The governance in India has never come up with radical policies and programmes to bridge this gap. Elected politicians hardly visit their constituent people at the ground level to see what they are doing and what problems they meet with and how they could help them. These tasks are apparently left to the *panchayats*. The elected representatives are concerned more with creating a rapport with the rich and powerful individuals in the leadership of governance and their associates in the corporate world, so as to enhance their own influence and power.

Much talked about are airy phrases like "Unity in Diversity", "secularism" and "national integration". These clichés do not make much sense for the common people. The reality for them is that there are different castes, different religions, and different ethnic groups living adjacent to each other, but certainly not helping each other in making their lives better and in creating a sense of unity. These cliches do not take into account the heterogeneity of the poor in terms of caste and ethnicity norms, religious beliefs and social class behaviour. Different social groups live side by side in a haphazard manner. In the urban areas, slums existing alongside the railway tracks and highways adjoin huge mansions. These slums are mainly temporary habitations of migrants who come probably to work at the construction sites which are a few yards away from their slums. These migrant labourers may visit the same market place, as the rich in thus mansions and the same railway station, but they maintain their social distances as they are from different castes and ethnic groups.

If we examine the socio-economic background of the persons manning the bureaucracy in India, they are generally the educated intelligentsia of the country, namely, those who have access to higher education and are professionals. Many of them are highly cued in the art of diplomacy. They are distinguished by being called "*Sahibs*", when male, and "madams', when female, as distinct in rank from the messenger who sits outside their offices, carrying files from one office to another. The latter are distinguished by being lowly when compared to the clerk of the office, who himself is lower in status to the bureaucrat belonging to the upper echelons of governance. The bureaucracy is in-charge of managing and implementing policies and programmes. A person in the higher echelons of bureaucracy wields much power and status. He can call any person working under him at any time, give quantities of work and if pleased with him, raise their status and if displeased may transfer him. The attitude of an underling in the bureaucratic hierarchy is to be subservient to the persons above him, for he thinks his main duty is to please his boss. Most of the time doing exactly what one is told by the boss is the custom, whether the boss is right or wrong. It is only in rare cases that the efficiency, competency, initiative and innovativeness of the lower class individuals are appreciated.

There is little conscious and transparent interaction between the people manning the Government and the people for whom the developmental programmes are to be planned, budgeted and implemented. The majority of the poor who are illiterate and live in far-flung places see the politician only when he goes on tours or is the speaker for an event for them with the usual marigold garlands. These visits of the politician are understood by the poor as having something to do with some benefits for them, but what in actual fact happens is a full stop after the visit is over. The poor are unaware of what is called the Planning Commission and the various Departments of the government. They are only knowledgeable about which politician represent their area or who is the *Panchayat* President or the District Collector within their geographical environment, since the poor are mostly agriculturists working as casual labourers on other people's farms or in mines or in forests and hardly come in contact with those in governance living in cities. The statutory figures in the government, except those who are their immediate representatives, are also little known to the poor. In times of need, the *Sarkari* people are sought after for assistance in getting jobs, transfers, higher grades or sorting out any glitches in their work environment through their representatives who belong to their *baraadri* (extended family). It does not make much difference to the politician's constituents as to his character, whether he is money-making or honest and ethical, so long as he gets their jobs done even though they might have to pay some commission for them. Frequently, the politician has more power than the bureaucrat to change the circumstances of the poor, for bribery is a very powerful tool. A *Panchayat Pradhan* who is a local level politician typically owns much property, belongs to the upper caste, and is more or less the overlord in his own group and is the one who has the "approach" to the bureaucrat in his constituency. He is therefore approached by the members of the constituency who know him well to plead their cause before the bureaucrats who matter. Since the poor have nothing to give in recompense to the politician representing them, they would render services just as a feudal underling did for the *zamindars* as in the days of the old feudal regimes.

Added to the variable of being either a bureaucrat or a politician, is the predominance of the variable of wealth. A wealthy person can bargain for change in his situation using his wealth as a means of bribery and hence it follows that the wealthy, usually belonging to the upper castes and the educated, had and still continue to have control over the poor. In short, and ironically, the old *jajman* system has only changed hats.

The question is which power has got the upper hand: the power arising from position in the governance or the power arising from economic wealth. It has not been unusual that from the time this county had proclaimed democracy as its form of governance, a covert system of bribery has continued in some form or the other. Thus, when a poor man does a job for the upper castes or class, he usually tends to say" *"mere chai paani ke liye kuch chahiye"* ("give me something for my tea and water"), which is a euphemistic way of reminding the upper class lord for a recompense.

This system of giving and taking favours has now found its correct niche in what is now familiarly known as "corruption". The term "corruption" or *"Bhashtrachar"* implies non-ethical behaviour and violation of the trust people put in those they have voted to power, mainly the politicians and in those who have been selected to manage their affairs in governance, namely, the government officials who are in cohort with the politician in the constituency. "Corruption" has now grown into a full-blown abscess in the nexus of the politician, the bureaucrat and the corporate world. The ones at the lower rung have the least power and the least wealth and are the most voiceless. But, fortunately, a civic society group has emerged in 2010 in the middle class to speak for the poor and when the civic society speaks with one voice in many parts of the country for the removal of corruption, they are in a sense voicing the fears of the poor who suffer the most by such corrupt activities. This suffering is mainly due to the fact that corruption, big or small, is in fact depleting the developmental budget for the uplift of the poor by surreptitious pilferages. The corrupt are pocketing these developmental funds without any qualms.

After the civic society group termed the "Team" it raised the issue of corruption and demanded the institution of a strong Lokpal, which was talked about for several years but had never been implemented, there was awakening of the average person or *aam admi* against the corrupt ways of politicians and bureaucrats. Almost everybody who is not ensconced in positions of political and bureaucratic power has joined the cause of the civic society led by Anna Hazare. They reasoned that if everybody, irrespective of whether he is a king or beggar, is under the jurisdiction of an independent watch-dog body against corruption consisting of worthy people to judge those who are corrupt and to advocate their punishment, then there would be some semblance of honesty.

Consequent upon the popularity of demand for a Jan Lokpal Bill, there is also a heating up of finger-pointing by one Party at another where every occasion is sought by one party to degrade other parties and, therefore, by implication to indicate how upright one's own party is. Feeling the pressure from the civic society groups, the Government under United Progressive Alliance led by Congress, finally had to come up with a Bill in the Parliament's winter session of 2011 but the provisions in the Bill introduced in the Parliament was not up to the expectations of the civic society group. The Bill was also opposed by the Opposition parties as well as some of the political Parties. This opposition also was further enhanced because of the infringement on state rights, if the Central Lokpal Bill provides for "Lokayuktas" to be appointed for each State. Such resentments have also been expressed by the different non-Congress State Governments on different other issues such as setting up a National Counter Terrorism Center (NCTC), which, as many Chief Ministers of States had alleged, had not been previously discussed with them. The stand of the major governing Parties has made it amply clear that they are disinclined to bring in a Lokpal Bill. For, if such a Bill was introduced, it would involve the "merry makers" of the major governance as to their takeoff on misutilisation of developmental funds.

In some sophisticated bureaucratic offices, the-drawers of the tables of the high and highly are kept open invitingly which are understood as being "fillers for the coffer". Most people in rural areas know the power of the *Pradhan*, the power of the judicial magistrate and the power of the District Collector. People are used to appeasing these powerful officers to get what they want. This is evident in what we commonly hear people say to such powerful people: *"aap hi sahib mere zindagi bana sakte hain"* (Sir, only you can make my life worthwhile), *"Saheb, aap mere bete ke liye ek sarkari naukri dila dijiye"* (Sir, please find a Government job for my son). It is, therefore, not unusual to find that programmes like *"Garibi Hatao"*, the National Rural Employment Guarantee Scheme, have all been poorly implemented simply because of their misuse by those who have more power and more open drawers at the upper crust level. For instance, a *Panchayat Pradhan*, who is supposed to manage and oversee the implementation of these programmes at the local level, most commonly skims away part of the benefits from the rightful beneficiaries, whether the issue dealt with subsidies or with the giving of seed money or the subsidizing of entrepreneurial activity.

Thus, we see that in the cognitive scheme of things the people manning the administration have their own agenda and the politicians their own. Powerful members of the corporate world abet the corrupt ways of the politicians and bureaucrats for their own favours. Caught in this web of the three power holders, the uneducated, the ignorant villager, who lives by his daily craft, whether he is a small farmer, a fisherman or a tribal forest produce gatherer, live their lives by depending upon the vagaries of nature and by whatever they get in return for their hard labour from rich managers. The existential conditions of the poor farmers and tribal people have been further adversely affected by the policies. Here the govenment favours the rich on the issue of land acquisition for grabbing the land of the poor.

Such policies of the Government favouring the rich and neglecting the advancement of the poor make India a perpetually poor country in the sense that the vast majority of its people continue to remain poor. This is in sharp contrast to the situation that we should be aspiring for. Inspite of the controversies about the correctness of the argument of Thomas Sowell, the scenario that he presents about the situation in America is the one that we should aspire for and that situation is as follows:

In America, "most of the people in the bottom 20 per cent of the income distribution in 1975 have also been in the top 20 per cent at some point since then. People who are genuinely poor all their lives still exist, but only about 3 per cent of the American population remains in the bottom 20 per cent for as long as a decade" (Sowell, Thomas, 2000).

Can this scenario be possible in the Indian situation? The answer will be discouraging unless the governance in India changes to move to empower the vast majority of the poor with assets and capabilities for participating in the wealth creation as co-equal members of the society.

REFERENCES

Express News Service, "3 per cent dip in infant mortality rate", *Indian Express*, 30.12.2011.

International Institute for Population Sciences (IPS) and Macro International, 2007, *National Family Health Survedy* (NFHS-3), 2005-06. India: Vol. 1, Mumabi: IIPS.

Margaret, C. Hogan, *et al.*, 2010, Maternal mortality for 181 countries, 1980—2008: a systematic, analysis of progress towards Millennium Development Goal 5, *Lancet*, Volume 375, Issue No. 9726.

Masud, Nadai & Yontcheva, Boariana, 2005, *Does Foreign Aid Reduce Poverty?*, IMF Working Paper (WP/05/100), IMF Institute.

News in Times X channel on Television on 9.5.2010.

"Poverty in India" reported at http://www.economywatch.com/indianeconomy/poverty-in-india.html

Sonalde B. Desai, Dubey Amaresh, Joshi B.L., Sen Mitali, Sheriff Abusaleh and Vanneman Reeve, 2010, *Human Development in India: Challenges for a Society in Transition*. New Delhi: Oxford University Press, p. 20.

Sowell, Thomas, 2000, "Perennial Economic Fallacies," *Jewish World Review*, 07 February 2000, http://www.jewishworldreview.com/cols/sowell020700.asp, accessed 03 January 2012.

UNICEF, 2009, *The State of World's Children.*

7

Linkages among Global Demographic and Economic Factors affecting the Indian Poor

The analysis in the previous chapters takes us straight to the concept of prevailing differences in living standards at all levels, whether it is global, national, State, town or village. In the Indian situation, differences have not changed drastically in the area of social patterns of living, but, gradually over the years the economic standards especially in the urban areas, have changed perceptibly. In the area of societal norms, socio-religious beliefs have hardly changed (Saraswathi, T. S., & Pai, S., 2000). For example, for generations it has been thought that children are God-given and families welcomed a large number of children. In this era, this attitude still continues, especially among rural and tribal traditional families. There is an increase in population as it is a socio-religious norm that families should have sons for the performance of religious rites and, therefore, more children are welcomed, even though covertly amniocenteses take place when a family has too many girls and does not want another female so much so that village men bring their pregnant wives to the nearby towns where ultrasounds can be performed so that they can have abortions done if the fetus is known to be a female. As said before, patriarchy is the prevailing structure of the families where the male is the head of the household and the female the *second sex*, and therefore, the patriarch is the final decision-maker (Ganesh, K., 1999). This is unlike the prevailing norms in the western democratic counties where egalitarianism prevails. Therefore, a major difference is in the socio-cultural area.

It is in the economic sphere that attitudes and values are similar. In fact, for the past last two decades or so, imitation of western ways is valued to the extent that the imitation exceeds the model, especially among the *nouveau riche*. This is especially true for the younger generation who wish to acquire wealth as soon and as much as is possible, for which the young generation values higher education, professional and business skills. The seeking after new avenues of wealth has been triggered off by international exchanges of technical, technological and innovative skills. A fairly large number of Indian professionals are working in the west and a fairly large number are in international trade and commerce. There are several multinational organisations working in cooperation with their counterparts in India also. This economic interaction has led to migration of Indian professionals to the west as manpower is abundant in India in comparison to countries of the west.

If we look at the global scenario of development, there still continues to be the economic and political dominance of the developed countries over the less developed eastern countries. There continues to be a control of the poorer countries by the dominant western countries, especially the most powerful among them, by means of restricted trade and commerce and imposition of sanctions. This strategy of taking control of the poor eastern countries, in most cases, is an excuse for entering into the dynamics of the poor countries so as to accrue benefits of having access to their energy sources. We do not have to go too far to witness this. The western powers have imposed sanctions against North Korea and Iran for the curtailment of nuclear power development by them. This is ironic since the developed western world itself has nuclear power stock piles. We have witnessed western countries deploying such strategies in the Middle East countries of Iraq and Libya. In Libya, with the successful removal of its autocratic leader, it may be possible that this is a good entry point for the western world to have access to its oil resources. One such example of entrance into India by foreign powers is the entry of FDI into retail markets.

India entered into the international arena of the WTO and forums of the UN and now into the G20 group of nations. China is now donning the mantle of leadership of the Non-Aligned countries. There is no doubt that China is the acknowledged most economically rich and technologically developed country among those striving to hold the topmost position of global leadership. There is no doubt that such fora as the UN, NATO, EEU and such like western dominated groups are using their powers to intervene in the sovereignty of other less powerful nations (Rochester J. Martin, 2006).

This kind of global behaviour of domination of the powerful western countries over the developing counties is also reflected in India, where there are States like Maharashtra and Gujarat which are more prosperous in industry and agrarian products, while others are hovering on the brink of near survival like the newly formed states of Chhattisgarh and Jharkhand. There are in place what is called "regulations" and "controls" imposed by the central government so as to attempt to neutralize the power of the rich over the poor States by creating subsidies and incentives for the latter, which so far have not been speedy enough to close the distance.

The most high-profiled threat nationally as well as internationally, is the fear of terrorism. In India there is also militancy in the form of the Naxalite or Maoist movement and disturbances which cause destabilization in the poorer States. On the northern border, there are several anti-Indian militants fighting for the annexation of the Kashmir valley. These are constant factors which are kept in check by a large force of the army and border police. Again, there are frequent skirmishes along the LOC (the line of control). These smaller internal groups are constantly to be guarded against and therefore cost the exchequer a large yearly sum of expenditure. Consequently this causes a cut in the budget meant for infrastructure and other development programmes which could benefit the poor.

Now that India has joined the high table of G20, there seems to be some confusion as to what it wants from it and is mostly reactive rather than proactive. Also, in some respects, India's revenues seem to have been placed in the wrong slots when construction like building infrastructure takes place. For, it becomes common knowledge that monies are siphoned off by those who are entrusted with the construction and what evidently occurs are poorly constructed cheap facilities which do not last long such as village schools, primary health-centers and such like.

The recent mismanagement of funds for the Common-wealth

Games held in Delhi in 2010 is a case in point. During the building of the commonwealth infrastructure, the poor living in shanties, under bridges, along the roadsides, were all forcibly evacuated to their places of origin in villages and tribal areas so as to present a "clean" picture to the international visitors. Now with the ending of the Commonwealth Games, it is business as usual. Like little ants, these disbanded poor have returned to their original places of habitation, under bridges and in shanty towns.

Effective leadership that is transparent and responsible is the *sine-qua-non* of good governance. Unfortunately, there are many worms in the woodwork of current governance as was before and will probably continue to be so. It is evident that unless there is a commitment to the education of the poor and creation of skills in them, every other effort will, so to speak "tend to sag to the floor". Unless there is a change in the values of the leadership, the situation will continue to be grim (Wakhlu, Arun, 2012).

So, we can observe a relationship between power and economic wealth. The Indian polity is more geared towards inter-activity with the international world of trade and commerce, signing MOUs, treaties, attending international conferences, visiting international meets, inviting and honoring international leaders in which much time, effort and money goes, but which does not result in anything of the sort that would redress the plight of the poor. This is because eventually, the fruits of these international interactions accrue more to the coffers of those in high profile. However widely stretched are the revenues, there is health-care in state-owned hospitals in India, even though poor in infrastructure and personal, in contrast to the rich developed USA where health insurance is often beyond the affordability of those who are not able to buy insurance. This is even more so after the recession of 2008 has rendered many Americans jobless, who are usually on the dole of social security. In contrast, in India it is mainly its large population which is diluting the effects of the implementation of subsidized government care in health and education, which is stalling the provision for all.

In other words, India has all the trappings to become a progressive nation, but its progressively enlarging population, especially among the poor, decimates the availability of prompt and good services for them. The developed countries can spread their revenue to reach more people mainly because they have smaller and more homogeneous populations, and because a large number of them pay taxes, which is not similarly reflected in the Indian society, as only a miniscule are employed in permanent jobs and are therefore taxed. In fact the Scandinavian countries have little or no growth rate in their populations because the fertility rate is almost nil and, therefore, they are able to prosper.

The attempt of global powers to hold in captivity the poorer nations is not a new phenomenon by itself. It is repeated in human nature everywhere. The less powerful have to submit to the more powerful, whether a country, a State or a district or a province or a community group.

The word freedom has to be taken in context. An individual cannot have the so-called freedom unless it is also shared by others to the same measure within the same contextual frame. In India, we are witnessing a disproportionate rise in investment in property where there is freedom to own more by the richer. Unless there is a reasonable restriction to the term freedom to be accessible to the total population, there will continue to be some who are less free than others and this applies more so to the poor and the powerless. It stands to reason that the more one has to invest in a profit-making enterprise, the richer the individual will tend to become. So, freedom has to be taken in the context of social groups that co-habit the same space as the other social groups and have an equal opportunity to access the same amenities as do the others. For example, the up and coming phenomenon of land acquisition by industries depletes the wealth of the poor farmers who are forced to sell their lands at a mere pittance, and not having any other skill, move to the already crowded slums in metropolitan areas in search for casual labour.

Thus, we see that as the global world shrinks in terms of communication and services, there is more telescoping of activities and the effects of one territory has far reaching consequences on the others. This happens from country to country, within States in the countries and amongst individuals in the cities, towns and villages. The closer one territory is to another, the greater the impact. The impact of the voted politician to his constituency and its constituents in policy making and the bureaucrat in relationship to his departmental work is a social reality in Indian governance. In these situations, each group facilitates the other due to nepotism and corruption.

Henry R. Nau describes the interactions among terrorism, human security, development, civil society, global governance and political economy. His main thesis indicates the continuous linkages between one and another phenomenon. (Henry R. Nau, 2010).

The global world is composed of countries with varying ideologies, socio-religious beliefs and levels of wealth. Each one has a long-standing existence in power or powerlessness which describes its political stature. The existence of the developed and powerful western countries seems to have sway in many of the forums that concerns international politics and law. It is, however, essential to know that there are some countries like those in Latin America which are beset with problem of drugs. Many African countries are afflicted with the problem of conflicts between varying tribes and the Middle East countries have to cope with the problem of religious fundamentalism and militancy. Other countries in Asia, especially South East Asia, have a more philosophical approach to life and live more or less peacefully with their neighbours.

Among the developed countries of the west, there is a covert struggle for supremacy of one over the other. Further, there are also convergences as in their attempts to participate in international fora like NATO, EU and the different other Groupings, namely, G-7 and G-20 (Lawrence S. Graham; Robert C. Grady; George Joffe; Alan M. Wachman; Donley T. Studlar; Richard P. Farkas, 2006). From a dispassionate point of view, they all seem to want to achieve the same thing that is domination of one over the other in a subtle manner. There are several countries, for instance, in the European Union which are going bankrupt and are only shored up by being bailed out by other members of the Union. There are even discussions as to whether the EU should use a single monetary currency as it keeps destabilizing and reviving in a very unpredictable manner. With them are also vagaries that are happening in the west, with regard to their economic systems and the fact that there are global inter-linkages with the east and Far-East. There are also destabilised situations in the European countries and its fallout has repercussions on the east and Far East countries.

The fundamental question raised by Orlando Albornoz in his book Sociology and the Third World Perspective (Orlando

Albornoz, 1992) is that, essentially Eurocentric/Western theoretical and the paradigmatic base of the social sciences today may or may not be consonant with current third world realities.

In the past decades, India was fairly isolated from the world events, with little interaction with western counties as is the situation currently. India was outside the realm of dynamic events taking place, both overtly and covertly, among nations of the world. Its major interactive countries were Russia, USA and the UK, which had different ideological systems of governance in their countries. With the end of the cold war between the erstwhile Soviet Union and the US, and the coming of various international and national trade agreements like WTO, free trade was accelerated between India and the Western world, especially the USA, where India did much outsourcing for American organisations. Currently, India obtains its oil from the Middle East, technology from the West, and with China, there are various deals, especially in technology and nuclear sciences. However, everything is not a rosy picture. With Pakistan not being able to contain terrorists located in camps in far-off places within that country, India has experienced several terrorist events and loss of life even though the line of control is being well-guarded. With the USA, India has signed deals for the buying of new warfare machinery and equipments, when the US President Obama recently visited India; and when Cameron, the Prime Minister of U.K. visited China, he did the same in trying to sell their goods to India and Indonesia. This is an ironical situation where there is a juxtaposition as to who is the taker and who is the giver. It usually is that the developing countries take the initiative to buy from the western world, and here we have the Western world moving out of its sphere of interaction to initiate selling equipment to eastern countries. These changes in positioning are not without its repercussions for then what India is doing is to build up its nuclear and biotechnological status in relation to other countries. This does not help the poor, because this heightening technology relating mainly to warfare materials does not have any effect on the lives of the poor. It only relates to shoring up of the defense status of India versus China, which in a sense is dangerous as any spark between India and China might lead to confrontations. Instead one could say that the money spent on defense and warfare could have easily been curtailed and the budget could have been reassessed to give more to health and education for its poor.

India is also attracted towards procuring the latest war equipments so as to be near par with China and other countries which might endanger its security such as a constant back and forth with Pakistan. This tendency towards acquisition of warfare equipments is perhaps dependent upon the need for protection of the country from damages that might be caused by militants or from other countries, and yet we have to ask the question as to what is more important. The rise of China, which is euphemistically termed "the crouching dragon", its unique position in being perhaps the greatest creditor to an economically recessive America, its expansion in many areas, especially defense and its close community of highly productive labour, presents a highly competitive threat to its neighbours including India.

So there are many divides among and between nations because of the economic recession and as how to manage it in terms of creation of jobs and economizing on consumption in almost all countries. However, the west has not been used to an eastern economy that shows its claws to a western world. For this reason it might be totally unprepared for confrontations with the east. As it is, America is beholden to China for the great part of its debt. However, these high level politics are of little utility for the poor in India. Recently, the Prime Minister of India in one of the meetings of the Summit Meeting held at Bali, Indonesia, in Mid-November, 2011 was optimistically cautious when he said that whatever cooperation that would take place "would be within the four walls of the law of the country", and yet at the same time, in fact almost immediately deals have been signed with America for nuclear equipments for India.

Ironically, it is now much clear that what was usually charitably called the poor South, namely, the African and Asian countries, and the erstwhile charity-giving North, namely, Britain, Europe, North America, are now dynamically changing their positions in view of the bright scenario of GDP in the eastern countries. It seems that the shoe is on the other foot and it is predicted that in the near future, both the dollar and the Euro would have lessened values in relation to other currencies in the east.

With this changing global scenario, the middle class in India is growing in a healthy fashion. However, the rising middle class of people who are in better paying job situations than in the last decades, lack the quality of skills, the work ethic and the commitment to quality products. Till such time as this quality is competitive with that of the westernized countries, it will still lag behind in terms of marketing its own products vis-à-vis other countries. There is much potential of skills in the Indian population that is relatively poor, that their enhancement would imply not only the production of quality products but also the opportunity for increase in jobs and, therefore, standards of living.

Now that adults in urban India are increasingly using the cellular and the internet for communication, the possibility of enhancing their world-wide knowledge is increasing. What is lacking is perhaps the social wealth which include better relationships among ethnic groups, less caste discriminations and more interactions in regionalism with better education and health. These are yet to happen. Therefore, whatever strands of globalization affect India it is necessary that the benefits should reach the poorer. Otherwise we will find situations where farmers are displaced by technology and where casual unskilled labour is increasing. It is said that with the internet intending to spread its network into most village panchayats, communication and information would be speedier than before, although one must admit that if the intended clients are not educated they may not understand what is written on the internet unless there is a constant interpreter present in the panchayat. The focus of a few villages being on the internet in their village panchayat is not representative of the whole and does not automatically indicate that such internet information is available to farmers, even if it is at the district level since almost all farmers are unused to computer language and are mostly illiterate.

We have indicated in the pages above that policies are in place, yet their strategies of implementation are mostly non-aligned with the practical needs of the poor. As said by a high-profiled politician, there is a policy paralysis in India. Therefore, the intended target group is tangentially touched and there is little ownership of policies that are poorly implemented. In most cases, the poor, at the best, receive a small proportion of the intended budgetary allocations. This is inspite of the fact that the poverty alleviation programmes have sung their song for the past 50 years. Currently, there is talk about the passing of a food security bill which will be a very heavy expenditure on the exchequer. It may be difficult to cover everybody who needs even the small amount of food grain as the bill focuses on. As a point in case we give the following illustration: A young woman from Jharkhand working as a domestic maid in Delhi when asked why there are so many poor people in Jharkhand, she had this to say: "I come from an Adivasi tribe, where our land is becoming less fertile, and unlike the rich farmers on the plains who receive all kinds of Government help, we hardly see this kind of help as much of our land is being usurped by rich industrial people." Indeed, we see this kind of usurpation currently going on in Greater Noida, Uttar Pradesh between the agriculturists and the rich industrialists who want to use their land for construction. This happens to be significant for there are several parts in the country, where industry is expanding and therefore encroaching upon rural lands. This is done by displacing farmers, by buying their farm lands for pittances of money, inspite of the fact that there is a land acquisition Act, which prohibits such under-cutting, in payment for the land that is bought. Currently, there are scams about land transactions initiated by State Governments and Netajis who buy rich lands for less money. In addition to displacing the poor from rural areas, there is a big business in picking up helpless rural people to work in urban areas on construction sites at exploitative rates, paying them less than what they deserve. The woman from Jharkhand continued:

> "We were told that there would be district hospital in every district, but that is only talk. Many of these centers are opened with one or two people, while the midwife earns her money in going from job to job in the village and the doctor has his private clinic, which he pays more attention to. So I thought life would be better if I took a job in a city, but yet I miss my family, my mother is not well and my father is not able to earn much, therefore, I have to send most of my earnings back home for their upkeep." She continued. "if my parents had received Government help and if they had a good school and a good health centre, there would have been no need for me to come in search of jobs to cities where I hear that young girls are often badly treated. We have to manage here as best as we can. Many of us are falling ill when we do not get jobs immediately, or when we are laid off. In the face of this, it

> follows that the money which is meant for us poor villagers as promised by our politicians goes elsewhere, but hardly come to help us in our farming activity, even though our farms are small we could live off the land but now we have to buy almost everything."

At the country level, the recent 2G Spectrum scam which came to light through media probing has revealed that about Rs. 1,76,379 crores have been missing from the Government exchequer because of the allocation of 2 G Spectrum licenses at throwaway prices to favoured industrialists by a political- bureaucratic nexus, where the excess assumedly was pocketed. Similarly, there are other scams belonging to the same mould.

The National Sample Survey Organisation (NSSO) has estimated that the unemployment rate grew exponentially in 2009-10 to 9.4 per cent from 2.8 per cent in 2007. Even among the employed, only 15.6 per cent have a regular salary and 51 per cent belong to the so-called self-employed category (National Sample Survey Organisation, 2011).

Again, the National Family Health Survey — 3 (NFHS) has shown a worrisome decline in health standards compared to the findings of NFHS-2. The former shows that the percentage of children aged between 6 to 35 months suffering from anaemia rose from 74.2 to 79.2 per cent. For married women in the age group of 15 to 49, anaemia rose from 51.8 to 56.2 per cent (International Institute for Population Sciences (IPS) and Macro International, 2007).

Gone are the days of dependency on food subsidies from other countries. In fact, India has advanced so far as to be able to export its IT products to other developed countries. So what ails India that it still has somewhere between 60 to 77 per cent living on an average of about Rs. 20 a day?

It is all very well to hear high sounding deals of billions of dollars in transferring nuclear energy, in trade agreements with economically developed fast-paced countries and of India getting a position in the UN Security Council. The real matter strikes home that even after two decades of increasing technology and increasing facilities, there are still millions living at sustenance level. Therefore, what causes the economic differences between the rich and the poor? Besides the facts that we have indicated about the congruence of poverty with illiteracy, with lack of basic essentials, and belonging to the lower castes, which are more or less excluded in the development process, what else contributes to this wide difference between the poor and the less poor? One might take a guess and point out to the various tax havens in which black money is stashed away by unscrupulous politicians, bureaucrats and businessmen: the unholy tri-nexus. It is said that if all the black money was returned to India and fairly distributed among the poor, there would be very little poverty as of now.

In analyzing the present scenario, the main problem seems to be human nature and the way the average Indian is attuned to somewhat unethical ways of acquisition of wealth. This occurs either by bribe-giving or bribe-taking or what is worse taking commissions for themselves from monies meant for the development of the poor.

The poor are hidden away in villages, in inaccessible hilly areas and coastal areas, which are far-away from the bureaucratic hubs of business activities which are often the domain of the better off. The cause of their rights and privileges can only be expressed on a one-to-one basis with Governance by the "civic society" (the coherent and righteous minded middle class sections of society) who can speak the same parliamentary language as does the politician, which the poor cannot. Several villages are outside the pale of these so-called technological improvements so that even after these two decades of rising GDP, not much has changed for the poor.

Developmental programmes will continue to be a social facade as it is very much like the feudal overlords giving charity to the poor. Therefore, human nature has not changed much over the last generations under feudalism and colonialism because of the values instilled in the individual where the upper classes and castes can accrue wealth to themselves at the cost of the lower. This is a curious irony because, according to the scriptures and the teachings that emanate from them, individuals in the Hindu ideology are supposed to be compassionate and sharing. This is not apparent. If at all there is any giving it is by the very rich who want to be tax-exempted, but at the same wanting to be shown as doing charity, like opening up hospitals and educational institutions in the names of the rich who are the "givers". Thus, the problem lies with the ethics, the civic sense of the people, irrespective of caste, creed, religion and ethnic divisions.

How does one help the poor populace overcome these differences among the classes? Firstly, ingrained in the lives of individuals from early childhood, irrespective of differences in caste, class or religion, there is a self-centered ethos. This is difficult to eradicate or minimize. This implies both child and parent learning about accepting these differences in the civic sense.

We have witnessed in our lifetime several incidents of ignoring the principles which call for an ethos recognised and practised by all similarly. For instance, there is much adulteration of food items, poor quality goods and services about which there is little protest. In other words, bribery, lower standards of doing the right thing are ingrained in the Indian psyche, emanating from a carry over of feudal values from the past. It is important to show that one is respectful, considerate and kind towards others, both in thought and action. However, this is hardly exhibited in the attitude of the rich towards the poor. Unfortunately one learns by imitation; children imitate their adults and so little ethical behaviour and attitudes are transferred from one generation to another. It is not an easy proposition since the majority of the people are not at the same level in understanding civics, ethics and law and order and their importance. In fact, non-ethical behaviour begins from the top leadership. Children by imitating grown ups become more easily unethical in values, behaviour and attitudes.

So instead of concentrating on childhood education, one should emphasize adult education in social learning situations, which then can be imitated by the young. Unfortunately, parents are not interested or have no time for being educated in social life-skills.

Further, since there are many widespread programs like the ICDS, agricultural education, teaching skills as in entrepreneurial enterprises, ethics can be introduced as a life program, emphasizing such values. Again, incentives should be given for those who mostly abide by civic rules, as is done by the reward system in schools. These, however, cannot be mass homogenous programs, but they can be introduced in small groups by people willing to participate. There is no dearth of finding innovative programmes involving both parent and child so that the child learns to imitate social values by imitating the adult.

Once again, in an overall manner, there should be programmes for training cadres of political parties, who should be inducted into these principles and whose conduct should be monitored in the social situations by the people themselves for whom these programmes are intended. This would, therefore, inculcate a sense of responsibility and accountability. Currently, evaluation of programmes refers strictly to evaluation by outsiders to present voluminous evaluation reports to bureaucrats. The desk reviews to which the bureaucrats are used to are accepted as sacrosanct and further planning is done on the basis of these lopsided reports, thereby reinstituting the same kind of mismanagement strategies. We have observed in the west that civic and ethical rules are spontaneously followed since it is a part of the culture, and the transgression of law and order is strictly penalized. In the developed countries like in the west, we have observed that where there are dishonest or unethical ways displayed by professionals, they can be easily sued and penalized by the judiciary. Hence, there is a great awareness in these countries of ethical public behaviour, unlike many parts in India.

Without the ethical foundation being tied to socio-religious norms, there might be little impact, and, therefore, the teachings of the scriptures and their practices must be related to secular values so that the Indian can easily see the relationship between the meaning of truth in the scriptures and the meaning of truth in secular behaviour. Unfortunately, the interpretation is made in such a way as not to destabilize the Governance where there is non-ethical implementation of developmental strategies. This non-ethical enactment is by connivance among the politicians, the bureaucrats and the corporate world. The corporate world is ready to sponsor unethical politicians in lieu of "payback from the political world". Such paybacks come in the form of favours such as granting of licenses. Thus, in a very covert way the *jajmani* system seems to have persisted over the years. Unless the uprighteous leadership insists strictly on ethical standards in governance, the same *jajmani* will continue. Ethical strategies will probably take a generation to be fully established, but a beginning has to be made somewhere instead of being lost in critiques.

Therefore, what is being done by the right thinking citizens to inculcate such thinking? One example, which seems to take a bigger shape, is the debate on the misuse of governmental funds. A frank analysis is just beginning by the educated and the experienced, especially the professionals of the middle class. The much debated Lokpal bill has been off and on the screen by the interested parties like a ping pong game for the past decades.

The executive or the bureaucracy, executes the plans biased towards their donors. Thus, there is a firm bond between the three actors which continue for each specific period of the rule of the voted politicians. Policies have been tabled, discussed, rejected, rewritten and re-discussed. When implemented they are mismanaged. Perhaps, it is not impossible to predict that the same might be the fate of the Lokpal Bill. This, however, requires overseeing by a highly ethical leadership or team; and the likelihood is that the same game will continue when discussed over and over again *ad nauseam*. There is no guarantee that the overseer leaders are themselves free from unethical activities, for it seems to be an ingrained attitude. No matter what the development programme may be, there is always the possibility of siphoning of the part of the expenditure by those who institute the program, maintain its progress and report on it. If such is the condition that the leaders themselves are involved in the corruption web, wherein corruption exists in an open manner, it is only left to the imagination as to what happens to the poor ruled by them.

However, all is not black clouds, there are now beginnings being made to unravel such scams and find out the source of criminality which have been cleverly manipulated by the hand-in-hand unscrupulousness of polity and bureaucracy. Unfortunately, in all this mess, it seems that the top level leaders of governance seem to have lost the ability to act quickly and bring about solutions. They seem content to hide behind the veils of holding committee meetings after meetings, writing and rewriting drafts which contain huge paralysed action. The poor, on the other hand, if they commit mild transgressions, meekly submit to whatever the authority say, because they know of no other alternative, or because they do not want to get into confrontation with the officials lest they are deprived of certain other privileges which are in the hands of these authorities. It is well-known that even in metropolitan areas, water pipes are broken into and water is stolen, that electricity is stolen, that anything left open to the public eye will certainly be pilfered. Such being the case, if we narrow down this scenario to the social reality of the poor, all these economic transactions at the high level involving nuclear technology, information technology and other technologies will only benefit the rich and the same is true of the rich in rural areas. Politics is such that people who are powerful like the textile mill owners, steel mill owners, large agricultural commercial farmers and such like industrial people are lords at election times. They use as much money as they can for election propaganda and for buying of votes, so that they are voted in, because being voted in as a politician especially at the centre gives them the opportunity to wield power over the powerless poor and make money. The voter has a mistaken notion that politician/politicians whom they vote into power are their saviors for redressing their grievances. This is an unfortunate delusion. For, these politicians will voice their own voices and those of their relatives and social networks and certainly not that of the poor man who is destined to work in unskilled intermittent casual labour. The axiom here is that while the rich get richer, the poor get poorer in terms of the distribution of the revenue that accrues to the Government. "Equal opportunities", imply that the rich have to share their benefits with the poor which they are generally unwilling to do. If one were to drive along the highway, one can come across large industrial complexes, steel mills, equipment-making factories which usually have large temples at their gates. The eyes of the passersby will be blinded by the fact that these are god-fearing honest industries, whereas it is well-known that it is a clever game played skillfully by the rich owners of such industries to evade taxes. The poor not paying taxes are not aware of such schemes. The wealthy industrialist thinks that creating such temples or giving money in charity will appease the godheads. It stands to reason that the poorer the geographical area, the less well it is catered to by the Governance. Not that the money set aside for development programmes is left by the wayside, but the strategies of mishandling of these monies occur at the operational level, indicating that there is inadequate monitoring and evaluation of how the money is being spent. Therefore, the money meant for the development of the poor goes into the pockets of the more powerful, especially those who are in the political arena, since they call the shots.

REFERENCES

Ganesh, K., 1999, 'Patrilineal structure and agency of women: Issues in gendered socialisation', in T.S. Saraswati (ed.), *Culture, Socialisation and Human Development*. pp. 242-43. New Delhi: Sage Publications.

Henry R. Nau (ed.), 2010, *International Relations in Perspective: A Reader*. Washington: George Washington University, pp. 747.

International Institute for Population Sciences (IPS) and Macro International, 2007, National Family Health Survedy (NFHS-3), 2005-06. India: Vol. 1, Mumabi: IIPS.

Lawrence S. Graham; Robert C. Grady; George Joffe; Alan M. Wachman; Donley T. Studlar; Richard P. Farkas, 2006, *The Politics of Governing: A Comparative Introduction*: Washington DC, CQ Press, pp. 323.

National Sample Survey Organisation, June 2011, Key Indicators of Employment and Unemployment in India 2009-2010. National Statistical Organisation.

Orlando Albornoz, 1992, *Sociology and the third world perspective*. Wiley Eastern, pp. 99.

Rochester J. Martin, 2006, *Between Peril and Promise: The Politics of International Law*. St. Louis: University of Missouri, pp. 198.

Saraswathi, T. S., & Pai, S., 2000, 'Socialisation in the Indian context', in H.S.R. Kao and D. Sinha (eds.), *Asian Perspectives on Psychology*, pp. 74-109. New Delhi: Sage.

Wakhlu, Arun, 2012, "Remembering Our Wholeness", in E. Sreedharan and Bharat Wakhlu (eds.), *Restoring Values: Keys to Integrity, Ethical Behaviour and Good Governance*. New Delhi, Sage Publications.

8

A Current Perspective and A Probable Future

Unless the policy-makers address the structural sources of the problem, which create and perpetuate poverty, the problem of poverty will continue to stay in some degree or the other (Sobhan, Rehman, 2010). As stated by the Foundation for Restoration of National Values, inactivity would push India downhill [E.Sreedharan and Bharat Wakhlu (eds.), 2012].

In this the early years of the 21st century, "the voice of the people", belonging to the average middle class is being expressed by some activist and intellectual leaders. Their concerted voices demand justice and equality for all, which in our context implies also the poor majority. They demand the stamping out of corruption and the return of black money stashed away in safe havens abroad. These are two of the most important current issues the governance in India is confronted with. There seems to be some ascendance of the voice of such people through what is now being called the "civic society" initiative.

Consequent to the unearthing of the high-profile corruption cases like the scams relating to the Commonwealth Games, 2010 held in Delhi and the allocation of 2-G spectrum licenses, there was a clamor from a group of people representing the educated middle-class "civic society" for the enactment of a law for setting up of a powerful Lokpal institution. The demand for such an authority had existed in the annals of the history of Independent India for many decades, but the political class has always succeeded in the past in scuttling the enactment of a law in this regard although draft Bills were prepared and presented in the

Parliament for discussions several times over. Because of the pressure that the "civic society" group could exert on the Government, the Government again came up with a draft Lokpal Bill in 2010 August. The Government's draft Bill was criticized by the civic society group as very weak and powerless and, therefore, insufficient to prevent corruption. They proposed an alternative Jan Lokpal Bill with strong provisions for penalizing the corrupt politicians and bureaucrats, including even the Prime Minister within the ambit of the supervisory authority of the Lokpal. The civic society kept mounting their pressure on the Government to adopt the Jan Lokpal Bill in Toto. The political parties opposing the Government also utilized the occasion to corner the Government on the issue of corruption. The Government at last brought up a "Lokpal and Lokayukta Bill, 2011" and got it passed by the lower House of the Parliament, namely, the Lok Sabha on the 27th December, 2011. However, when the Bill then went to the upper House of the Parliament, the Rajya Sabha, where the ruling party did not command a majority, its passage was again aborted mainly because some of the regional political parties led by an alliance partner in the ruling alliance (namely, the UPA) objected to the provision of Lokayuktas for States in this Central legislation as, according to them, this provision was contrary to the principle of federalism.

There is a saying that "a leopard cannot change its spots". Likewise, the general demeanor of a political party or a politician might just as well continue to be what it always was in the past decades. What will happen in the future is anybody's guess. Perhaps, this repeated failure is because if the Bill was to be implemented, it will cause many heads of the polity to tumble. While it is admitted that several in the governance are ethical and come from uprighteous backgrounds, there are disturbing elements in the system of the polity which take advantage and under cover delve into corrupt and devious ways of under-cutting sustainable development for the poor by siphoning off budgetary allocations meant for them.

The efforts of political parties who are aiming to be in the chair after the next general elections are now piping the same pipe against corruption inspite of the fact that it is well-known that many in different parties have been involved in scams of various types. Some in the polity have been jailed, some have been let out on bail and still others are being pulled into the dragnet of the searchlight of the judiciary, many of them being politicians at higher levels. Therefore, there is a slashing back and forth of a long drawn-out rhetoric on all sides with an ambiguous commitment of the elected to institute a "Grievance Addressal System". The non-elected argue that if the elected are not performing their functions in the interest of those who voted them into power, namely, the masses, then the actions of the latter become dysfunctional. It seems ironical to use this term "non-electables", does it mean the "lower castes" or "females" or what is called the segment that is known as "miscreants" (people with criminal histories). It does not seem to be so. For, there are now elected three female Chief Ministers who seem very vocal that their point of view should be upheld in the governance milieu. For example, the Chief Minister of West Bengal is very focused on decimating the Maoists in the northeast of Bengal.She has now left the UPA Government. What is her objective outside this realm is hard to gauge. The Chief Minister of Tamil Nadu is implementing justice against the old cases of corruption. It is well-known that the Congress will have a large stake in Uttar Pradesh at the time of the general Parliamentary elections to be held in 2014. The Samajwadi Party has taken over the governance of Uttar Pradesh in March, 2012 elections. This Samajwadi Party has a large electoral support base which is much prized for its voting capacity in the general elections and is being woed by several of the powerful national parties whose hopes are set on the forthcoming general elections in 2014. This does not exclude Narendra Modi of Gujarat jostling to stand at the helm.

Since the winter session of Parliament, 2011, several Chief Ministers have been questioned about their non-ethical actions so that as elections draw nearer, there are ding-dong battles going on. Who is trying to prove what, why, and? how is it shrouded in mystery. "Criminally-intentioned" characteristics of many of the elected representatives are hidden and unknown to the general public. It must be admitted that social and electronic media are creating a greater awareness amongst the general public and, therefore, it is becoming difficult for the corrupt to hide their dubious activities. Even at this juncture, for example, a Cabinet Minister in a State has been questioned about his fidelity. However, we are experiencing the rising and vocalizing middle class Indians in protest against the criminalization of the polity. The ruling governance is, therefore, in a tight corner as the voice of the people ask for answers to their questions relating to what we now term the *"corruptible"*, whether in the corporate world or the bureaucracy or, what is more significant, in the polity, and their right to information.

On the other hand, if there are individual cases of criminality, especially against the powerless, namely, the middle class and the poor, there is little possibility of redress since they are unable to afford legal redress or to find ways and means to tackle the corruption. It is well-known that the poor suffer from many disabilities such as domestic violence for which although an Act has been recently constituted not much is done to redress the grievance of the poor abused women, nor is there much attempt to legalise steps against prostitution as several in the polity at all levels would prefer to be in control of the situation.

It is also known that it is possible that bribe-giving and bribe-taking occur throughout the hierarchy of the polity and bureaucracy, but since one does not know whether the next person is a bribe-taker or a bribe-giver, everybody continues to accept the situation "as is where is". The poor tolerate the situation as they have no recourse to any kind of help except in rare cases where some NGO volunteers assist these harassed groups. The "elected" tend to ignore such cases and sit in parliamentary fora making airy speeches or watching pornography during sessions.

Therefore, if the constitutional directives of equality and justice exist, they do so only in name for the majority of the poor, who are also the disadvantaged, the marginalized and the powerless. They are not in high profile in the minds of the elected polity except perhaps at the time of elections when their votes are important. For example, there had been a hypocritical scramble for appeasing the group of "Backward Classes" among Muslims by giving them a sub-quota of 4.5 per cent within the 27 per cent reservation given to the "Backward Classes" in Government jobs and in admissions to educational institutions.

As is well-known, India, with the rest of the world, is in the throes of recession with one saving grace. This is because, by Government policy, it did not deal with non-registered banks, paper money (i.e., credit cards) or with heavy dependence upon mortgages and bank loans. Most of the poor and the lower middle class kept whatever little they had in family gold as a measure of security. Although India is not in heavy recession, the adverse effects of the global recession are hurting the people in poor circumstances the most. These poor people constitute nearly three-quarters of the population. Under global recessionary pressure, India's GDP growth rate fell to 6.7 per cent in 2012 from an average of 8.8 per cent growth rate witnessed from 2004 to 2007. Though this decline was nothing like the recession faced by the West, the 2.1 per cent decline in India's GDP growth rate had effectively translated into a 2.8 per cent increase in the incidence of poverty as estimated by the United Nations Department of Economic and Social Affairs (UNDESA) (Srinivasan, Rukmini, 2010).

The global recession is a wake up call for India to realize that it must stand on its own feet and develop the skills of its people rather than being dependent for their developmental programmes on donor assistance from the developed countries, which themselves are now affected by the recession. India operationally while being a democratic country as it subscribes to the tenets of democracy, in real terms it is more of a social welfare state. This seems a curious juxtaposition, because, on the one hand, India has adopted wholesale the ideology of the west, namely, democracy, and superimposed it on a society which had for generations lived under a feudalistic social order, which unfortunately has left its mark. In the years prior to Independence, there was a systemic relationship between the ruler and the ruled. The rulers had all the powers and the ruled were in subservience living on the magnanimity of the rulers, and abiding by their autocratic regulations. A kind of ideology existed which indicated that the overlords looked after those whom they ruled, whether in a magnanimous way as did Akbar or in an indifferent way as did the British colonists. Now, suddenly, the country is being exposed to the world of democracy which it little understands and which is much less practised.

India operationally is unable to fulfill the components of the ideology that they have adopted since they were not and are still not prepared to react to them in the way the British did, the Americans do and other democracies are beginning to do, as no other country has this heavy burden of differential caste society. The ideologies of several emerging nations are different, but by global interaction they could either benefit or confront each other depending upon their "hidden agendas".

With these varying ideologies and strategies among these countries, wherein each have their own covert intentions, India is sitting between two stools. One stool is the continuance of the traditional system, involving *jajmani* and casteism, inherited over the years which tended to create discrimination and yet, currently, on the other hand, incredulously sits on the new cushion of "freedom" and "equality". At this juncture, in the last quarter of 2012, the Parties are playing an earnest chess game with each other, sitting around chess tables, concentrating as to who will be ousted and who will be the next player.

It seems that in India, it is the wealthy, the knowledgeable and the artful who orchestrate the strategies of development which are only tangential to the poor. In this situation, the majority of the poor will continue to be less educated than the rich and less knowledgeable about the world of nations around them. As a consequence, they are also economically powerless in relation to the relatively minute number of the rich elite, the powerful politicians, the powerful bureaucrats and the wealthy corporate world. It is in the interest of the nexus of these latter three that the distance between them and the poor continues to be maintained, especially since there are no measures for population reduction and it is well-known that the population of the poor increases at a faster rate than does the population of the rich. If the poor were to become well educated and, therefore, aware of their Constitutional rights and privileges, they could have more quickly become knowledgeable about the machinations of the nexus of the politician, the bureaucrat and the corporate world, and become articulate in demanding their rights and privileges as happens in democratic countries where civic rights are due to everybody irrespective of power or position. Even as of now it is still the middle class that is voicing their rights and privileges for the poor. So far we have seen that the economic wealth and the power of governance are in the hands of the nexus of powerful politicians, bureaucrats and the corporate and the poor are outside the pale.

In this state of affairs, it is absolutely essential that the Governance recovers the monies from the tax havens of the rich and utilizes them for the purpose for which it is meant, namely, the development of the poor majority. This should be done in an honest, transparent and responsible manner. If the politicians are to be true to what is said when they take the oath as Members of Parliament, then they should be truthful to the people whom they represent and work in their interests. It almost seems as if the politicians who are dishonest have split-personalities: one face that is shown to the voters and one face in the realm of parliamentary and programme affairs where they operate with their hidden agendas.

The lack of honesty of the elected and trusted members is evident from the fact that they could not do anything effective and tangible about the reported unaccounted wealth of the 700 Indians stashed away in tax havens in Swiss and other banks. It has been reported (http://taxguru.in/finance/swiss-bank-revealed-indian-have-more-money-then-rest-of-the-world.html) that, according to the Swiss Banking Association Report, 2006, India tops the list for black money in the entire world with reportedly $1456 billions in Swiss Banks.

The social reality in India is that the poor also wish their children to be as educated and knowledgeable as much as do the rich but have suppressed this desire as they do not have the means or the opportunity and have to work for their survival. The right to education, however, which has been stagnating over the decades, is still being stymied by those in power. The political representatives want the poor to continue to be underfoot and, therefore, are not as committed as they should be in persuading their constituency bureaucrats at all levels to see that the children of the poor are at least in the school. At the central level the governance is more interested in obtaining technology and nuclear power to compete with other countries and less interested in the welfare of the poor. It is not too late, although many opportunities have gone past, that the Government in a transparent fashion avoids corruption and implements programmes such that governance works in the interest of bettering the quality of life of the poor whom they supposedly represent. However, the ultimate question is where and who are the non-corruptible elected who will deliver these services and facilities to the poor in a transparent, accountable and responsible manner? We do not know and perhaps will not know for a long time to come. If the poor continue to be poor, India will continue to be termed as a "developing nation" inspite of its growing GDP which unfortunately stays only with the elite.

It is true that corruption cannot be ruled out wholesale. The *Jajmani* system and the *Jati* system are deeply rooted in social values and attitudes of the people and, therefore, some "siphoning" of revenues will continue to occur. In fact, some form of this kind of corruption occurs in other countries also. However, it should be pre-empted at the beginning by the proper controlling devices and prevented by good governance. This will only happen if the revenues are ethically and judiciously managed. It is suggested that activities should be proactive rather than reactive in utilization of monies / subsidies / facilities for the poor. The village *panchayats* should participate more intensively in planning and building their own infrastructures and capacities like roads, wells, water management and such like. This is the true meaning of community participation and because of this involvement of the community, the products may be more efficiently and economically utilized, especially by the poor in the community. The community can provide the labour for their own developmental programmes, monitor their progress themselves, rather than looking to their representatives to do their work for them. Such is not the case presently, for the community leaves the work to the government agencies saying *"yeh, sarkari kaam hai"*, while the Governmental agencies do not perform the tasks as they should since their monitoring and evaluation is very superficial and mostly done as paper work by "desk workers". Therefore, vigorous, innovative and informed community participation is essential.

Unless these measures are implemented with a sense of commitment, there might be a leisurely attitude towards building these basic infrastructures and providing the planned facilities. We are very familiar with the all too frequent behaviour of individuals who put off the job to be done or adopt a leisurely attitude. These are *"Aisa Hi Hota Hai"* (it happens this way), *"Sab Kuch Hota Hai"* (everything happen this way), *"Chalta hai"* (it goes along like this) and such like phrases, implying an acceptance of delayed measure tactics in implementing schemes and a tolerance and haphazard attitude towards the poor implementation of schemes. This is an attitude born out of generations of accepting events as part of one's *"karma"* or fate. When crises occur, the effect is washed away by saying that "yeh *hamara kismet hai, yeh humare pichle janam ka karam hai*" (this is my fate, this is the bad luck of my previous birth) and such like sayings, which are regressive and absolves the individual from having to do anything on his own to improve the condition or taking responsibility for himself and for others. *The simple thesis, is therefore, only one: the continuance of one concept: namely, the poor in India will continue to be poor so long as the political governance does not mitigate their problems by the commitment to programme activities for sustainable development with a sense of work ethics.*

Indians are well-known to be great talkers and there are innumerable discussions, debates, fora and conventions. They all go round and round the mulberry bush and hardly get down to practical measures and implement them in a concerted and systematic manner with time-bound parameters. Indians are also known to be leisurely committed to the sense of time. Time in the west is like money, but in India the attitude towards time does not have the same boundaries.

What is required is that all people unequivocally understand their rights and privileges, and their relationship to the different aspects of polity, the administrative set-up, the meaning of the parliamentary system and the judiciary in dispensing law and order. Also required is an understanding of the role of the police in the maintenance of law and order which often needs strict supervision considering that they are not immune to bribe-taking.

As the financial year 2011-12 was drawing to a close, there were several bewildering things happening. A scam of "discretional allotment of coal blocks" was reported to have caused a loss of several Lakhs Crores of Rupees to the exchequer. Deposed Ministers, both Chief Ministers and Cabinet Ministers, were looking for ways and means to be reinstated as was in the case of Karnataka in March 2012. Some other Chief Ministers were clamouring for a greater profile in strength and power, while others were being steadily demoted. In this confusion worse-confounded, finger-pointing increased rapidly and many cases were being revived to add to the confusion.

It must be mentioned, however, that the observations made is the author's own assessment as to the pointers of all the preceding events that is causing the turmoil currently being faced by the political system. These events will continue so long as the nexus of the corporate world, the bureaucracy and the polity are ego-centric and hand-in-glove to perpetuate their self-interests inspite of their pious proclamations about the benefits for all from these trade offs.

When elections are round the corner, political fervour among different political parties will be spurred on. Some have gone at it in a planned projected manner such as in the case of the implementation of the land acquisition laws. Some others have gathered momentum such as the movement towards demand for a separate Telengana State in Andhra Pradesh and the move for division of Uttar Pradesh into four States. Others are asking for separate States such as Gorkha Land. These latter momentum have grown because of the increasing awareness of the "civic society" and its spokesmen who are spurred on to create an atmosphere of freedom of the mind and "direct talk about issues". What will eventually be the outcome of such planned or spontaneous and opportunistic movements? There is little doubt, however, that the growing voice of the middle-class will continue to create inroads into the governance of the polity. As has been said succinctly by the elected Chief Minister of Tamil Nadu, "The future is unknown and only time will tell". These uprisings indicate that the tide is turning against the nexus of corruption among the polity, the bureaucracy and the corporate world. But, whether the tide will succeed in washing away these malpractices is anybody's guess.

On this the 64th anniversary of India's independence, the country seems to be mired in the doldrums. As one politician said, the Government is affected by policy paralysis. Again, there is much rhetoric from the Government, talking mostly about past achievements but with little relationship as to how to take the country forward. There is much talk about signing of agreements, MOUs and such like instruments between the leaders of governance and other countries, but very little as to what is being done domestically in relation to those almost forgotten poor as the polity is only involved in slinging matches trying to prove their artificial commitment to "democratic ideas" when in actual fact most of the agendas of the polity are hidden. The civic society has raised its main banner, the Lokpal Bill, which has tottered and fallen as could have been predicted. The fact of the matter is that there will continue to be parallel layers of talk and act. There is a great deal of the airing of one's own ideas, sometime irrelevantly by the parliamentarians, but very little on how the parameters of the Bill should be implemented and who is ultimately responsible. It almost borders on the ridiculous, that assessments now relate to who can trust who to be non-corrupt. If the Prime Minister is under its jurisdiction and is to be indicted, who will be non-corrupt in this process? If popular leaders are to be indicted who will be the least who can be selected as a panel from the judiciary so that the judgment is clear and correct. These are the really nitty-gritty issues, but everybody is so caught up in talking about their own attributes so that very little attention has been paid to the operative aspects of the Lokpal Bill.

As has been said before, in India the largest proportion of the poor are in the larger Central States of India, sometimes called the "Hindi belt" and sometimes euphemistically called the "Cow belt". It is essential for the tri-nexus of polity, bureaucracy and the corporate world to see to it that this large poverty population is kept suppressed because if they are educated and enlightened, the nexus will lose its power. The nexus's secret will be wide open to the public eye and the so-called guardians of India's democracy are really continuing to protect their own images, for, raise in the status of the poor is a threat to the rich and powerful.

The main theme of the opposition, as to be expected, is that they will try their best to find fault with the ruling Party even if they are small issues and blow them up to gigantic proportions. The current governmental administration is very circumspect. While it is being shouted about in various fora, the administration tends to keep a low profile. Perhaps what has to be said will be said within the four walls of the Parliament. This game in the polity between the contending parties who want to rule will continue but it seems to be a sad commentary on all these activities that they do not figure in high profile for the poor who are the people for whom the government is really meant and where ironically the Government protests that their activities are all democratic in nature for all people. Unfortunately, the governance is only concerned about its own governance for its own propriety and the poor are swept under the carpet and forgotten till the time of the next elections when their votes suddenly become precious.

It is time now that, in all earnestness, egos should be forgotten and that activities should be concentrated upon and implemented in a socially realistic manner so that, leaders are judged by what they do and not by what they say they will do. The global world is itself undergoing a recessive period. Its fall-out is also felt in India although it is reported that it is not to the extent that it is in the western countries. The fact remains that inspite of all the talk about developmental programmes in India, there is not much corresponding results to indicate that they effectively sustain the development of the poor.

The sessions of the Parliament come and go without much work being done. Many Bills are pending. The country has not learned the lesson that it cannot be developed if a miniscule proportion of its population is bulging with excessive wealth and the rest are more or less either at a standstill in development or have increased in their "non-equality" status. We are seeing initial signs of this frustration and the possibility that this widening of the gap will continue to grow if the leaders do not desist from battering each other and in reality do what they are supposed to do, namely, develop the country, more especially its poor, which should be its pristine mandate.

No matter whichever Government comes into power, the same pattern of rhetoric, dismemberment and disconnect with the poor is expected to continue. That there is a margin of difference between the rich and the poor in all countries is acknowledged, but the fact is that in India this margin of difference which was already very wide may become wider. This disconnect unfortunately is not in tune with the lofty ideas of governance. Unless there is a greater awareness, a greater voice and some power given to the poor to participate in their destiny, the "game" will continue as before. Perhaps, it might be argued that India is too large a country, almost a continent, with an unstoppable population growth to take care of even within these sixty years, but it does not brood good for government in action that the number of the poor in India are still increasing.

There is no gainsaying that the various scams will eventually subside out of the public eye but they will be replaced by newer scams unless something drastic happens to really punish those at the top. We understand that the dramatic arrests of the top corrupt politicians have now been smoothened out to such a degree that most of them have been granted bail. But this does not brood good, for it means that those arrested and bailed out will now have time to "rearrange" the witnesses so that there is no adequate evidence at the time they will be put on trial and, therefore, there are greater chances of their being let out scot-free. For name's sake, about half a dozen Ministers were in various stages of being indicted, convicted, jailed and bailed, so much so that it has been jokingly said that a Parliamentary Five Star Hotel should be built in Tihar jail so as to accommodate the various bigwigs in jail!

Much has to be said about the media being a spokesperson for the bewildered middle class. Every event that is uncovered by the media is turned inside out, so that it may be directly observed by the general masses as to whether the political event is a scam or not. Over and above this, is the infighting in Parliament between the two main parties, so as to show one-upmanship for the purpose of appearing the cleaner of the two at the time of the forthcoming elections. Added to this, are the *Yatras* against corruption, undertaken by the leader of the opposition and fellow partymen so as to indicate their "good intentions" in preparation for the next elections.

It was no surprise that the judiciary sprung up into full course of action to examine the cases of corruption through a telescope, and so was able to indict many. Evidence came in the form of video recordings, tapped telephonic conversations and copies of letters, back and forth, from swindlers to the conniving Government officials and vice versa.

However, as time moves on, it is anybody's guess as to what further complexities will appear on the political horizon. There seems to be a growing number of strategies back and forth in order to deviate attention of the general public from the shortcomings of the Government. We need to admit here that the situation is not one of morality and high-sounding standards, but one of money and power that is presenting the drama on the huge theatre of political upheavals.

Another cause of concern is that inspite of protests from the civic society, the Government is unable to retrieve the huge wealth of black money from tax havens back to the exchequer for the use of programmes for the public. This is understandable since the black money mostly belongs to the polity and the corporate world. Uncovering black money will reveal their disguises.

We must ask ourselves that out of all these confusion worst confounded, what clarity will eventually appear? This is currently not known. It is like watching a horse race and betting on which horse will come first, depending upon the barriers, the handicaps and which horse would stumble and which horse would steer clear.

We have witnessed a series of upheavals in the governance which reveal that they are not committed to dealing with the problems of the poor. As the saying goes, the worms have been coming out of the woodwork in quick succession, almost new ones every week. There have been many political leaders including Chief Ministers who have been jailed for being involved in such scams. Unfortunately, these political leaders are the first stakeholders for upholding the transparency and honesty in governance.

Will it be just that the public will be spectators watching a drama? Or that some of the youngsters currently in the polity and are Parliament members will eventually replace the oldies and bring a fresh enthusiasm and honesty into governance? It is hoped that the upcoming younger generation will have more empathy with the plight of the poor and will not indulge only in rhetoric but will also implement what they promise. Somehow the middle class seem to have got a foothold on the ladder of knowledge and awareness of the shams and scams that are happening in the polity around them, but have not cued the poor to observe such deviations in the so-called democratic polity.

It is really an incredulous situation to understand how in a pluralistic society, where the majority are illiterate and know little of sophisticated concepts like equality, justice and fraternity, that they have a structural system which gives them the opportunity to pick out the person or persons they would like to represent them and their issues. During the freedom movement and at the time of Independence, it must be remembered, the only people who interacted with the British were those who were well-educated and knowledgeable. Some of the leaders were, in fact, educated in Britain itself. For example, Nehru, Gandhi, Patel and Jinnah were all well-conversant with the British system of governance and their cry for freedom was composed of the very elements of the British democracy. The structure they used to formulate their own government was the British system of parliamentary democracy, including the two Houses of the parliament, similar to the House of the Lords and the House of the Commons in Britain or the Upper and Lower Houses which in India are termed the Rajya Sabha and the Lok Sabha. Inspite of having a similar structure of democracy as in Great Britain and in the USA, the majority are not conversant with the variables in the system till date, namely, nearly 64 years after its incorporation into a system of governance. In the new system, there is adult franchise but the average Indian did not know how to use it and much less the poor and the disadvantaged. The poor only knew two things in order to contribute to the representation at the governance level. One was to pick out someone who they felt would work for them and the second was that on the election day, they will have to affix their thumb impression on an unknown paper, the language of which they did not understand, since they were mostly illiterate. We have stressed these to indicate that the average Indian and much more so the poor are living in two worlds: one known and the other un-known. The known is the traditional and the unknown is the modern.

The Gandhian values and ethics which prevailed at the beginning years of Independence have slowly been eroded by ego concerns and the greedy hands of the rich towards usurping most of the benefits of independence. The politicians felt that once they were voted in, there was no need to proceed and interact with those whom they represented. In other countries, where this system exists, there is always a rapport between the elected and those who elected them as in America.

It is essential to note how many of the programmes of the Government really assuaged the needs of the poor. The programmes for the poor like the various rural development programmes and poverty alleviation programmes were mainly programmes of food assistance and subsidy. The rapport and the involvement of the poor in these programmes was hardly reinforced. There was little emphasis on development of their skills, their opportunities and the reinforcement of their attributes by the elected polity. These programmes did not emphasize what they should have, namely, the participation of the people in their own development where they should be made to feel that they own their programme. If the skills of the poor had been developed so that they could take control of their own lives through the implementation of such semi-skilled professions as would enhance their monetary incomes, perhaps the poor would not be at such a standstill as they are currently, many of them below the poverty line living without basic essentials.

It is seen, therefore, from the overall perspective that programmes come and go, but the same type of politicians seem to go on, whether of one party or the other. It seems that the way of all politicians follow the same route. When they are in power, they push their agendas through; and when they are not, they obstruct the procedures and use delaying tactics for those bills and laws which did not favour them. This indicates that there is a lack of political will.

The advancement of Parliamentary democracy depends on programmes for improvement of infrastructure and the technical and professional abilities of its people. We know that several programmes for the poor are long-standing like the ICDS, the Food for Work, which have indifferent implementation and, therefore, end in less than the expected results. There should be innovative strategies which can compete with the social and technological changes in the world of today instead of continuing with the same old programmes which were not sufficiently effective.

One of the first bright spots in the Constitution of India was the adoption of the policy of free and compulsory education for primary school aged children. While the policy was recognized as an excellent move, it has still to be satisfactorily realized. Why is this so? Simply because the policy has existed without a structure and system that could successfully implement the action of this programme. We have only to look around District, Block and village schools to see how poorly they are managed with poor infrastructure, hardly trained personnel and without the interests of the governance.

We also know that in the demographic arena the productive segments of the population are being depleted in contrast to the growing numbers of the dependent population, like children and the aged. Further, there is an imbalance in the habitat in relation to its people. For example, because of technology being introduced in the farming methods and farm-land being bought up by industrialists, many young able-bodied village men migrate to urban areas in search of jobs, thus depleting the rural areas of their agricultural potential and overburdening the urban areas. This makes sustainable development precarious. It is not possible to make suggestions for every aspect of the operation of developmental programs of the Government, as most of them do not have total investment and commitment by the governance.

The real users of Government assistance are those at the household level, namely, women and children. In view of the demographic changes of increase in the dependent populations and the inability of the poor in learning the required skills to match the racing technology, it is essential that whatever programme implementation occurs, they should be high-profiled and directed toward households needs. Services are utilized realistically at the household level and perhaps more realistically utilized when given to the females of the family as it is they who care for the family members, especially in terms of nutrition and health. In real operational terms, the school should be brought to the child, the food should be given to the women and entrepreneurial skills should be developed at the household level. Women's participation in community programmes like community school and women's development programme is essential for development to take place at the grassroots level. For instance, in Ethiopia, which is a developing country and extremely poor at the village level, parents' cooperative nursery schools are proving to be successful mainly because mothers are also involved in participating in the activities of their children.

Neither the polity nor the bureaucrats are sufficiently interested in removing the barriers in the development of the poor. For example, in the provision of primary school services the fact that drop-outs are high, especially of females, indicates that something is wrong with the provision of services, especially as the females are considered the discounted "second sex". It is essential to remember that children will gain from primary school education only if they are interested or if parents reinforce their attendance or if it is related to the occupational skills of the family. This lack of reinforcement from the adults is probably because, at the end of the day, they realize that rote-learning or learning in geography and civic subjects does not help in improving the occupational skills of the poor. What the children need are learned skills related to the occupations available in their surroundings to participate in production of available resources.

It is important here to stress the significance of education for all children since it is basic and foundational for their understanding of the experiences they meet with in later life. The Government should reinforce the parents of children in the poverty sections to avail themselves of education that would be of use in later life, like for instance, technical and entrepreneurial activities.

In the paradigm below, at the first level we give the existing conditions, at the second level the intermediary interventions / interventionists and at the third level we make some tentative suggestions which are "do-able" like concentrating assistance for the poor at the household level. These do not cover the whole spectrum of sustainable development, but they concentrate on the most important measures, at the household level, because it is at the household level that the basics are required and that females in the households are the major ones to see that their children are nourished and educated and the household managed with the available income by the females. These measures will inadvertently also help raise the status of the female so that she can also participate in decision-making for the household.

Programmatic Assistance at the Household Level

Interventions
— Literacy
— Primary Education
— Healthcare
— Decreasing high infant and maternal mortality rates
— Increasing micro Credit and direct delivery of subsidies

Delivered By
1. Policy-makers/propellers
2. Field Agencies at the Grass root Level
3. Assistance in rural entrepreneurial activities by the corporate world

Suggested Measures	
Children	Vocational and Technical Education
Adults	Entrepreneurial and Simple Banking Knowledge
	Budgetary allocation
	Participation by knowledgeable female beneficiaries
	Revolving Bank Funds through rural banking systems

Since many males at the household level in these poor segments are also illiterate, do not have land, work as casual labourers, or at the most as sharecroppers, they in the absolute sense are not skilled. They, therefore, need to understand the rural banking system, where the budgetary allocations are first deposited and since there are several layers of government intermediaries, there is no reason why they should not be the first receivers of the credit/cash/subsidies. Such measures will cut down the possibilities of corrupt practices in the chain of the delivery of services. In short, what we are suggesting is that the bureaucratic process should be shortened, for, the longer the chain of bureaucratic processes, the more will be the siphoning off of the allocations meant for the development of the poor, who are less knowledgeable than the better off landholders.

The status of the poor will continued to be stalemated unless and until some drastic reversals of policies and strategies take place and unless there are committed and honest deliverers of the programmes for the poor. By this, we mean that the poor should realize the benefits of developmental programmes to its fullest extent, and even though corruption may not be mitigated to some extent, at least there will be knowledge even amongst the beneficiaries that inequalities should be eradicated and there should not be exclusion of the poor from the major benefits of developmental programmes.

Together with the minimization of corrupt practices, several situations of the poor could change. As regards education of children, according to the Census 2001, nearly Sixty-five million children aged 6-14 years were found to be out of school (Global March Against Child Labour, 2006). This is unacceptable. These figures contradict the claim of the Government under *Sarva Shiksha Abhiyan* (Education for All) when the Government's Education Department states that only 25 million children are out of school. Such contradictory claim is what makes it difficult to plan programs for the children of the poor on a realistic basis and unless children have a proper education, they cannot take the future into their own hands, and, therefore, when different figures appear from different sources on the same variable like education, it throws the whole system of planning out of gear.

The uplift of the poor cannot be just giving them opportunities for steady labour or just educating children in the three "R"s (a widely-used abbreviation for the basic elements of a primary school curriculum: *reading, 'riting (writing), and 'rithmetic (arithmetic)*, but there should be a combination of these factors so that the levels of poverty are depressed in this large proportion of the poor. If this lacuna is not mitigated to the fullest extent possible, with the underlying foundation that the implementers are transparently honest and accountable, then there will continue to be a large proportion of the population that is poor and further still the growing population that is below the poverty line.

Coupled with the lack of education for children, we have unvaryingly low levels of nutritional intake amongst poor sections and undoubtedly for those under the poverty line. There is as yet no proper food security for them and only promises for job opportunities. Therefore, lack of education, lack of food and lack of job opportunities together stranglehold a large majority of the future generations, namely, the young people, who have to take over the leadership of the country in an honest and ethical manner (Yusuf Sayed, Mamya Subramanian, Crain Soundien, Nazir Carrim, *et.al.*, 2007).

If this is the condition in this 21st century, exacerbated by the corrupt practices of the leaders in the bureaucracy, the polity and the corporate world, we can easily extrapolate that the latter three will fight tooth and nail to protect their interests and their hold on the economy and power, and more so depress the implementation of policies for the poor, especially in health, education and creation of jobs. There is no reason why inspite of the proclamation of policies of health and education for all that such a large segment of the poor get bypassed with little redress to realign them into the mainstream of inclusion and advancement. Why are these policies depressed in actuality? Does it mean that there is indifference in implementation or that the budgetary allocation is not adequate or not completely used or that it is diverted elsewhere? This diversion is yet unknown and, therefore, the all-enveloping question arises as to why after more than half a century, the poor are still poor who are relentlessly increasing in absolute numbers.

Unfortunately, the fact is that the Budget allocations for health and education are much below that of the budgetary allocations for defense and industrial development, indicating misplaced priorities. The poor will then have to fall back on different types of unskilled or semi-skilled labour. Added to this saddening phenomenon is that between 41-47 per cent of the population are dependent upon the productive population of those of the young who are earning (Government of India, 2001). The latter, however, are mostly in the upper and middle socio-economic classes.

Currently appearing on the Indian scene of the divisiveness in the polity is the factor of priorities. The Government is still oriented outwards towards interactive international activities. Naturally, this interaction is with the western world of give and take. The United States does not have the requisite skilled manpower to accomplish their technical work and so outsourcing is in fact less expensive for them and advertising their own sales is another area of interaction which is euphemistically called "economic cooperation". The sense and sensibility of turning the eye inward is still yet not fully realized. One such incident that has recently occurred is the attempt of the Government of India to allow Foreign Direct Investment (FDI) in the area of retail marketing. It is propounded that the expansion of the extraneous retail market into India will also assist the Indian producers to the extent that infrastructure will be built for the marketing of their produce. However, what is more important is building the domestic infrastructure, namely, abilities and facilities of the producers before entertaining foreign investors which will grab the local markets and push under the carpet the local producers. We have seen this happen in the days after India entered into WTO. Goods from Taiwan, China and other counties are at a price much below that of local production and, therefore, undercut domestic producers. Not that India needs to import large stocks of food grain. Shockingly there are many tonnes of wheat bags lying in the open as there is insufficient storage infrastructure. Therefore, why not maintain one's own produce and create infrastructure that preserves them? There is also the fact that many thousands of tonnes have rotted because of untimely rains.

It is well-known that where technology is introduced, there is displacement of manual labour and this technology can be conducted by a smaller number of people with better expertise of running large projects. We have, noticed how Reliance retail shops have not been as popular as the traditional markets. In the latter the bring in items are brought into the market everyday and usually dispose of the same day. India is still traditional in its food systems like the way the food is bought, stored, cleaned and used from time to time as far as grains are concerned and a great value is placed on getting fresh food items from the closeby markets almost everyday. This is a pattern of food culture which would be hard to displace and, therefore, the outcome of sophisticated systems vis-à-vis the traditional system in food and other living habits have yet to be assessed as regards their merits, especially for the poor. This is the general feeling of the poorer classes towards such sophisticated enterprises. The poor in rural and tribal areas are tangential to the growing sophisticated malls in urban areas. Left on the backburner are such important issues as education, health, hygiene and preventive measures to reduce IMR, MMR, anaemia, malnutrition and such like deficiencies.

India has always been dubbed as an economically poor country, not because it does not have vast resources, but because they are relatively untapped for the largest proportion of the population, namely, the poor. In the face of this insecurity, the poor become vulnerable to the machinations of the upper classes. Therefore, the basic premise of the reduction of poverty continues to be in the lives of the rural, the tribal and the urban poor, where resources are scarce.

If comparisons are made between India and China it may be seen that in 1947 the average annual income in India was US$439, compared with US$619 for China; but by 1999, the numbers were US$1,818 and US$3,259 for each of these countries respectively. It must be remembered, however, that these figures represented a time when these two countries had moved gradually into the arena of liberalisation and globalization, thus increasing the GDP of both countries, but hidden under this statement is the fact that the high per capita income is more indicative of the rich rather than the poor and also it is said that compared to 2009 the GDP of India has dropped by two points in 2011. Thus, it is really not known where this growing GDP has gone to. Perhaps, one might surmise the part of it has gone into black money for the purpose of buying and giving bribes for cash for votes and for obtaining licenses and lobbying, all these activities being labelled corrupt.

The poor in India are still beset by lowered rates of food intake in terms of calories. The Median Monthly Per Capita Calorie Consumption in India, which was 64,056 in 1987/88 has come down to 62,917 in 1999/2000 (Chatterjee, Srikanta, Allan Rae and Ranjan Ray, 2007). The percentage of malnourished increased not only because of the high birth rate among the poor but also because of the fact that the rural areas were persuaded by the governance to invest in cash commercial crops as it brought in greater revenues which naturally depleted the land available for foodgrain cultivation. This fact was further exacerbated by the farmers who had to sell at government prices and who, therefore, realised less for themselves than before in terms of food. The Government introduced the PDS system to shore up the lack of food availability for the poor. However, mismanagement, adulteration and black-marketeering indicated that the PDS shops declared that they had less stock than they actually had. As the country gave more heed to industrialisation and world trade, food availability in rural areas had lessened to such an extent that many farmers gave up food cultivation, moved to cash crop cultivation or to seeking jobs in urban areas (Patnaik, Utsa, 2006).

Regarding food nutrition which is the most basic of all necessities, it is said that the highest rate of malnutrition in the world is in India. An estimated 42.5 per cent of children under five years in India suffer from malnutrition, undoubtedly, mostly from the poorer sections of the society (Sengupta, Somini, March 13, 2009). This has long-term consequences for the physical growth, development and productivity of young people who will make up the future leaders. We do not have to look too far to know that food is being imported from nearby countries like that prompted by recent crisis in onion availability, the poor man's vegetable. Naturally, with the increase in the prices of staple foods, the rural poor will eat less than they should.

In the face of the above, what do poverty alleviation programmes really do to reduce the prevailing poverty status of the majority of Indians, especially in basic essentials? Starting from the community development programmes and through a host of other programmes mentioned earlier, the fact remains that the rush for occupations in the industrial sector depletes the rural household of its labour productivity. It is true because of this emphasis on earning cash in urban areas and entrepreneurial activities, there has been a rise in the numbers of the middle class, but that is only a miniscule number since they are a class in the service sector, while the rural poor have to find ways and means of earning a survival livelihood. The miniscule rich are over-abundantly supplied in their wants while the middle class is slowly climbing up the same ladder not far behind. Therefore, it is important to set our sights to the future and to know how much of food needs to be produced and sold at the rates affordable enough for the poor to buy.

We have moved away from using the term "community development" to a more comprehensive term "sustainable development" which implies a continuous and steady support by all involved within the parameters of the development situation with each individual contributing towards it. The efforts of all are mainly towards the maintenance and creation of energy and ecologically habitable environments. There are several examples of generation and preservation of energy which would not only be of assistance to poor farmers in arid areas, but also to the efforts of the total population in the given ecology to use energy for both farmers and non-farmers. This change in terminology does not imply desegregations, but in fact it implies aggregation as sustainability depends upon every one in the given population irrespective caste, ethnicity or social class contributing towards development. This can be done mainly by active participation in developmental programmes in which the poor reside and shoring them up so that full benefits are realized. There are several ways in which energy can be created. We already know of plants running on solar energy, of the creation of watersheds for water management and the use of cattle dung for the purpose of domestic cooking like biogas. Given the incentives by the Government, it is not difficult to persuade the enthusiastic young people, especially in rural and tribal areas, to use innovative ways by which they can obtain and sustain energy. In this process, there is no such thing as upper or lower castes. Anyone provided he has or she has the potential and the capacity, can invent, create and maintain entrepreneurial activities in energy conservation and enhancement.

There has been some debate on whether there should be emphasis on the development of the average in the demography or whether efforts should be concentrated on those below the poverty line. Both sides have a point (Ravallion, Martin, 2001). Though much of the data on development is an index of the average growth, we have to concede that the effect of the average trickles down to those below the average to some degree or the other. During the economic growth spurred by technological advancements, mobility occurs both geographically and vertically.

All individuals, whether from the poor or the middle class, or the upper classes, are striving to better their living standards and statuses. The one factor that differentiates among them is that the poor find it harder to move vertically in search of a better standard of living. There is not much data on how the GDP, which is an average index, affects the poor, but this much we know that, "other things being equal", the rich benefit more from the growing GDP than do the poor.

In education, it was estimated that 50.39 per cent of the students dropped-out by the time they reached the VIII standard in 2004-05 (Govt. of India, Ministry of Human Resources Development, 2005) Although official figures claim that there are 12.66 million children who are child labourers (Census, 2001 released in 2005), unofficial figures claim that if we add to this number the child labourers in agricultural and domestic sectors, the total would rise to 25 to 30 million. Also, unaccounted are street children and beggars who sell miscellaneous items at stop signs along the roads. These are outside the pale of the official child labour figures (Planning Commission data quoted in Global March Against Child Labour, 2006). All in all, it has been stated that, 260 million people, or 26 per cent of the population, live below the poverty line irrespective of whether they are casual labourers, child laborers or female labourers.

While this document has delineated the processes involved in the governance of the poor over a period of time, currently the concentration is on the improvement of each political Party for itself in the face of the forthcoming elections in 2014. It is assumed that after the elections, everything will come back to square one as before. The so-called poverty alleviation schemes will be diluted and desultory. In fact, finding a way out of the trenches of corruption seems to be the "success banner" of all Parties. Yet, it has not been specified as to corruption in what and where. Very little is known in terms of actualities. What is well-known is that corruption has increased by leaps and bounds. Everybody is elbowing everybody else out of the way even to the extent of castigating the other. We have watched debates where accusations back and forth come down to the level of personal incriminations. Parliamentary demeanour is forgotten to the extent that the old-fashioned parliamentary system adopted wholesale from the erstwhile rulers seems to be falling apart. It is lengthy, laborious and adopted in such a fashion that it seems to be not well understood even by the middle class, leave alone the poor. Sometimes, even politicians do not understand their own system. There seems to be a lack of understanding of how parliament should be conducted by the general group and a lack of good intentions to really put on the anvil the cause of the poor. Now it is the cause of the self at the expense of the other that is paramount. These are self-directed strategies and certainly not strategies in governance for the poor. While we may not be able to forecast what will happen in the future, one theme will continue, namely, the poor will be at the bottom of the rung and the alleviation strategies will remain more on paper and less in action, unless something unforeseen and drastic happens to change the demographic character of productivity of the population.

At mid-night on the 29th of December, 2011 every hope related to the institution of a Lokpal Bill came to an end in the Rajya Sabha when at the end of the acrimonious debates and discussions, about 187 amendments were proposed to the Bill which were impossible to be reconciled within the short period of time available in the session. It seemed inevitable that the major purpose was to somehow delay and scuttle its implementation, especially in view of the elections of 2014 which would display the corruptibility of the very polity itself. At that time, the opposition Party heckled the Speaker with irrelevant comments and one representative of a well-known Party even went to the extent of tearing up the Bill and flinging it on the floor of the House. One might say ironically that this gesture is what Parliamentary democracy is all about! The momentum of the fight of the civic society was suddenly snapped at 3.30 PM on the 29th December, 2011 when the civic society realized that the Bill was not being passed, and there would need to be alternative plans. These plans could include going to the States that were to have elections and preaching their slogan of anti-corruption. This did not happen. Currently, the movement of the civic society is still in the doldrums. In fact, one of the leaders of the civic society has disengaged himself from the civic society group and has formed a fourth political group. There are of course jeers and sneers as to how he would gather a political party and give it a resounding name. There is a saying that the more the merrier, and this is one such instance of confusion-creation. Thus, the morale of the movement has fallen and the huge tent of promises made by all Parties towards making a STRONG Lokpal Bill collapsed like a huge tent which has lost its fulcrum.

It is also been said that the movement of the civic society was one of peace and quiet and in that sense was exemplary of the true meaning of the philosophy of "*ahimsa*". In 1947, the Indian rulers donned on an unfitting garb of a democratic set-up, borrowed from the foreigners. They have struggled to contour it according to the requirements of the average Indian whose needs are simple and unsophisticated. It seems more and more clear that the adopted package of democracy needs to be contoured in a way suiting the masses of Indians who are at one and the same time traditional and yet moving towards modernisation. The essential principles of democracy should be worked in such a way that they are comprehensible by every individual in the society, rich or poor. In many ways the poor are perplexed about the workings of the parliamentary system, the system of voting, and the existence of multiplicity of political parties seeking their votes. Less still is their understanding of the working of the legislative and the judicial systems. Therefore, if one is living in a an ideological framework that one does not understand, it becomes difficult to know what one's rights and privileges are. These are legislative and judicial features which are difficult to comprehend by the average individual in one's everyday life and much less by the illiterate poor.

If the master-minders in governance hardly take cognizance of the social realities of the poor, expectations perhaps will not be successfully realized as often there is disjunct between promises and their implementation. The cause of the poor had most often been put on the backburner. It is the self-centred, divisive and covert activities of the ruling rich, in discrete collusion with actors in the corporate sector, and the manipulative policy makers who shift as the wind blows, that will perhaps continue till even after our generation has long since passed and gone.

With the proclamation of the general elections in five States in 2012, there was feverish activity in the community of "vote banks". The emphasis on corruption has done a right about-turn. The poor are once again hidden under the cover of another set of rules, namely, elections. In fact, if at all anything is to happen, there will be appeals made to them to vote for politicians who go around with much fanfare and promises. It is as if the problems with the poor never existed before and only at the time of the elections is there an interest, but only for their votes. Then, most electioneering speeches make promises but when the elections are over, the parties suffer from amnesia. Then gone with the wind are actions for raising the poor above the poverty line and the frenzy about corruption. As said before in this document, everything will be back to square one. So will it be in the future.

Social media is a very vibrant informant of the socio-intellectual happenings, among other things, in the Indian democracy. For example, in a televised debate in early January of 2012 on the branding of the Indian political democracy, the major conclusion arrived at was that India's democracy is uniquely its own. In other words, the impression that one gets is that India is certainly unique if one looks at its inheritance from the feudal days and its wholesale embracing of a set of Constitutional directives to which it was absolutely new. It seems that the need-achievement oriented, educated young entrepreneurs have taken the challenge of stamping India on the face of the global world as a unique pattern evolving its own special paradigm of democracy. This was only talked about in force by intellectuals and in the private sector by those who have a sophisticated knowledge of what democracy means in the Indian context. For this we think the paradigm that existed in the olden days of feudal autocracies and in the colonial days is now no longer tenable for India. It has evolved its own special paradigm where because of the freedom to invent, to create, to seek opportunities, the freedom to develop exists in the paradigm. Unfortunately, it seems to be accessible more to the upper socio-economic classes than to the lower classes who are mostly the poor. In other words, it seems that the kind of democracy we have, may be viewed as a 'social welfare democracy". There seems to be a voluminous growth that eventually will become explosive in the continued efforts of the middle class to better themselves to find the wider windows of enterprise, especially given the interactivity in the global arena. By implication, it means that India has to adopt its own dynamic paradigm which allows for the interaction of homogeneity, heterogeneity and interactivity of the striving of the young men and women who will be the new architects of tomorrow.

India's entry into the world of globalization in the beginning of the 1990s threw the doors open to the entry of multinational corporations in to India and diverted the leadership attention to the parameters of world trade where the outflow of Indian goods and products were sold to the developed world in a free trade market. Correspondingly the goods of the outside world came into India. The consequences of this movement towards interaction on a global sphere, while increasing the exchequer, had an adverse effect upon the original producers who then had to sell at competitive prices to the detriment of the producer, namely, the agriculturist, the small entrepreneurs and the labour force. While the phenomenon of outsourcing worked by providing from other countries jobs to those who were educated and technologically oriented in India, it at the same time discounted the unskilled poor. We do not have to go far to see what effect this could have when crops failed and farmers committed suicide as there was little elasticity in the sale of their products. According to Prof. Utsa Patnaik, "Neo-liberal policies fine-tuned to capitalist accumulation are increasing poverty, mass deprivation and unemployment. Besides it also undermined food security in India, because the "effects of the much higher levels of labour-displacing technology and of automation today in developing countries is to produce jobless growth" (Utsa Patnaik, "Poverty, Mass Deprivation Rising in Asia", The Hindu, 15-01-2012).

A great deal of events are taking place in the theatre of political drama. Evidently the rival political parties are gearing themselves for confrontation in outrivaling each other and proclaiming pious intentions. It is evident that these are all intended for the forthcoming general elections. It is well-known that the major rivals include the one which is currently sitting in the seat of governance at the Centre and the one who is now the major opposition party at the Centre. They are busy rebuilding their images in the eyes of the voters, mainly through selected TV channels where they display their moral intentions. It is a question of getting a majority of voters on their side even to the extent of placating the minorities whom they have ignored most of the time. Others are looking for leaders among the Scheduled Casts and Scheduled Tribes and the minority groups like the Muslims to canvass votes for them. There are many ways in which the big fish are looking around for small fish (the big parties looking for the smaller parties as allies who are also in the fray). It has now become a race to collect as many politicians from smaller political bodies so that they could strengthen their pull in a game of tug-of-war. Practically everyday is witnessing a new scenario of political activity. There is feverish running around to look for the exploited poor in attempting to bring them over to one's side, since the poor form the majority of voters. Thus, it is a game of numbers. Like any lottery play much depends upon how much of "taking" and "giving" occurs, for we know that when the time comes for the people to go to the polling booths, there will be hectic lobbying by the politicians and their henchmen to persuade the voters to vote for them. No party has the complete resources to draw more and more people into their net as it is money and its power that matter in drawing voters to one's side. On the threshold of the beginning of electioneering for the next general elections, a game of musical chairs has begun with much push and shout of the smaller parties by the larger including the drama that has occured for the new and now current president.

Amidst all these confusion, the Government at the Centre wants to set up a national anti-corruption bureau. Several of the States has risen up in anger as they were not consulted for the formation of such a bureau and felt sidelined. The Chief Ministers of these States contend that since India has a federal government, the States should be consulted and bypassing this is an infringement of their Constitutional powers. Just as Lalu Prasad tore up the Lokpal Bill in the well of the Parliament, so did Rahul Gandhi tear up the manifesto of the Samajwadi Party. To the average onlooker this is like a puppet play. On the surface is a struggle for "me" and "mine" with little thought to the actual problems at the ground level. More and more the leaders insult the poor by treating them as pawns in the voting business in order to gain ascendancy in numbers, so the poor have been turned into lifeless numbers along a chessboard, to be pushed here and there. There is no thought given to their livelihood. Perhaps a few Chief Ministers like those of Orissa and Bihar are really concerned with the voluminous amount of mishappenings in their States and are working at repressing them quietly. The usual response of the Central Government to the protests of the States who have been bypassed in the process of these selective proclamations is: "we have taken note of their protests and shall deal with them in due course". These protests have in them some validity because they state that India has a federal system and, therefore, anything that is a new ruling or regulation should have their consent. This is a tug-of war which the Centre hopes to smother by using Constitutional rules and regulations and Bills and so on to allay the fears of the States but in essence it seems they are moving towards forcing a situation to occur very much like balkanization in Europe where Europe was split into many tiny fragmented countries. Would India then become a federal state like America or have separate States as in the European Union. The year 2014 will show the varied turns the country will have taken before it reaches a state of semblance or dissemblance. Will it be a majority rule at the Centre, will it be a coalition rule at the Centre or will it be a hanging parliament?

In all these medley, nowhere is there some semblance of taking care of the problems of the poor as the priority task as expressed in their political principles. For example, the poor who have suffered in the Bhopal Gas tragedy have yet to be compensated. The DOW chemicals company responsible for the Bhopal tragedy as of date has not as yet recompensated the victims. The company has gone ahead and sponsored the Olympic Games inspite of the protest by the Indian Government. There is a still great deal of bitterness and anguish among the poor of Bhopal who have been much affected physically and mentally by the explosions in 1984.

Further, such incredulous incidents are taking place such as the viewing of pornographic material by some parliamentarians when sessions were taking place. This exhibits the amount of commitment to their stately work! Belonging to the BJP Party, they resigned from their Ministership but not from the Party and, therefore, the onlookers from the other parties have raised a hue and cry that resigning is not sufficient, that they should be expelled from the Party to teach others a lesson. Otherwise, a leisurely attitude will be given to such morally outrageous acts. Recently a top politician was defamed by his own driver by producing a CD showing him in a compromising situation with one of his female colleagues in his lawyer's chamber. And now we have a routine of rape cases in Haryana and elsewhere. Morally, therefore, the upholders of high standards are ripped off their facades. Such like incidents are many, indicating the preoccupation of the governance with other personal matters rather than on serious mandates for the redress of the grievances of the poor. We have given these illustrations to indicate the trend of action by the governance which is certainly not for the poor.

One of the latest scams that has involved huge sums of money is the scam related to the National Rural Health Mission in Uttar Pradesh. There seems to be a deep mystery surrounding this case where six officials of the State's Ministry of Health have been murdered, leaving no clue. So far there is very little knowledge of how the State Government is dealing with this situation.

In general, law abiding citizens in whichever State, and there are quite a few, are becoming appalled and what is worse, have lost their faith in the morality and obligations of the Government both at the Centre and in some States where scams have exploded.

Given below is a Table 8.1 indicating the various parties ruling in different States in order to point out the various strengths. The larger States in terms of the number of Constituencies are Uttar Pradesh, Andhra Pradesh, Maharashtra, Madhya Pradesh and Rajasthan. From the Table 8.1 it is obvious that the two major Parties, namely, the Congress and the BJP, have formed coalitions with other smaller Parties. For example, the BJP is the ruling Party in Gujarat and Madhya Pradesh while the Congress is the ruling Party in Rajasthan and Andhra Pradesh. In the States of Maharashtra and Kerala, the Congress Party rules in alliance with other Parties. The non-Congress, non-BJP Parties are ruling in the States of Uttar Pradesh, Orissa, Bihar, Punjab and West Bengal. This presents a rough picture that there are many permutations and combinations of Parties and their utility will only be known at the time of the forthcoming general elections.

India accepted liberalization with open arms as did all fast-moving countries. The major mistake was the lack of in-depth analysis in the case of its major producers, namely, agriculturists who employed casual labourers at the time of harvesting.

Before Liberalisation the seeds were provided by the Government. Following the deregulation dictated by the IMF, several seed processing units were closed down. The cost of seed per acre for farmers then shot up from Rs. 70 in 1991 to Rs. 1000 in 2005. Farmers fell into heavy debt, especially in States where liberalization was more actively followed as in the case of Andhra Pradesh and Maharashtra. Further, these small-scale farmers had to borrow heavily from the *Mahajans* and in despair some of them left their low-producing farming for other precarious jobs. This trend was accelerated by the inroads made by industrialisation on to their lands. While the GDP grew on an average by 6 per cent in

Table 8.1: Political Parties in the States and their Strengths

	Ruling Party+ coalition	*Total number of Constituencies*	*Congress*	*BJP*	*Others*
Andhra Pradesh 2009	Congress + League	294	157	2	TDP 90 PRP 18 Since Congress is the largest party with hardly any opposition to stand elections, the probability is that Congress will be the major constituencies. With once glitch, mainly the tug-of-war with the Telengana Rashtyra Samility Party which is still striving for a separate State in Andhra
Bihar 2010	JDU + BJP	243	4	91	JDU 115 This is a coalition and the likelihood is that they will continue to rule in the next elections at the State level
Gujarat 2007	BJP	181	59	117	The BJP being the ruling Party with a strong head in Narendra Modi, the likelihood is that they will continue as there does not seem to be any large contending party or ruler, that is as great a contender as Modi
Madhya Pradesh 2008	BJP	230	70	143	Since BJP is almost twice as much as Congress, the likelihood that they will form most of the constituents is probable.
Maharashtra 2009	Cong + NCP	288	69	54	Shiva Sena 62 The same likelihood of parties overcoming the Congress

(*Contd.*)

Table 8.1: (*Contd.*)

	Ruling Party+ coalition	*Total number of Constituencies*	*Congress*	*BJP*	*Others*
Orissa 2009	BJD	147	26	7	BJD 109 In all probability, the Janata Dal will rule the State again.
Rajasthan 2008	Congress	200	96	79	BSP 6 Since there are three parties and there coalitions are unknown any two might form the majority in the Constituencies.
Uttar Pradesh 2007	BSP	402	22	51	BSP 206; SP 97; RLD 10 The outcome of which party will win the most constituencies can only be a guestimate since elections currently taking place and there is much confrontation, especially between BSP and the SP about high-handedness and disorder.
Punjab 2007	SAD + BJP		44	19	SAD 48; Ind 5 The probability for the same numbers in the Constituencies of the SAD will likely to head the state ruling.
West Bengal 2011	TMC		42		TMC 184; LF 62 The elections to this State will take place in 2016 and it is improbable to offer a guestimate.
Kerala	Congress+	140	72		Left 69 Apparently, the history of constituencies shifting sides will continue to take place everytime of the elections. The probability is likely to be the same.

the past two decades since 1991, agriculture growth rate slowed down from 4.69 per cent in 1991 to 1.1 per cent in 2002-2003.

Liberalisation and globalisation also lifted duties and tariffs on imports. The free import of food and other farm products pushed down the prices of produce of Indian farmers. By the logic of the liberalisation policies, the credit available to farmers from nationalized banks was reduced to 10.3 per cent against the recommended target of 18 per cent (Saurabh Mishra, 2005, "Seeds of Ruin" at Down to Earth: Science and Environment Online, June 15, 2005). There was a sharp drop in agricultural growth from 4.69 per cent in 1991 to 2.06 per cent in 1997 (Directorate of Economics and Statistics, Department of Agriculture and Cooperation). As a result, though agriculture still employs 60 per cent of the Indian population today, it contributes only 20.6 per cent to the GDP (Isaac, 2005). The increased cost of inputs and reduced prices of farm products hit the small farmers the most leading to heavy indebtedness, loss of sustenance and led several farmers to commit suicide. Therefore, by inference entering into all these new negotiations like liberaralisation and WTO has made life for the poor farmers much more precarious than before and somewhat ironically interaction with global organisations has indeed affected the poor ruralites much more severely than before. Liberalisation was good for those countries which were already stable like USA and Europe. But when focused on the developing countries, this deregulation and free import destabilised the already poor illiterate and debt-ridden rural farming society.

We will derive here a few hypotheses from the above delineation which will remain hypothetical. The general voting public is neither rich nor middle class, and not even working class, but are large numbers of the poor below or just above the poverty line, who are looking out for handouts just as happens in the West, where father Christmas hands out treats to little children, getting them to promise to be good children. So also the two rivaling father Christmases, namely, the Congress and the BJP in India, who travel on their overburdened black money sledges from different parts of the West where their unaccounted money is carefully stashed. This untaxed, untold wealth is used by Party members standing for elections at the time of voting, so that they can cajole, persuade the poor waiting beggars along the curbs of the polling booths to exchange "cash for votes". Therefore, the primary criterian is money for numbers. This is our first hypothesis, namely, if you have money, money will talk. And when money brings in votes then the hypothesis is valid.

However, there are intervening variables. These may be clubbed together into caste, ethnicity and those who are related by the *jajmani* system. This clubbing indicates that there is a high probability that caste will vote for caste, ethnic community for ethnic community, relations among *jajmanis* and the uneducated illiterate for promise favours from their masters. This is our second hypothesis, namely, that these variables affect the lives of the poor.

The third hypothesis is the lobbyist criterion, where a whole host of lobbyists from different corporates, different industries, and different job givers will go around offering jobs to the poor for the purpose of voting their favoured politicians. Therefore, there is a close relationship between lobbying and their giving their favours to the poor voters.

Over-reaching all these, of course, is the average estimate of how well or how badly the Central Government has been estimated to have achieved what it has promised to achieve, especially in relation to the poor. Therefore, the next hypothesis is the relationship between government's efforts and the relief given to the poor by the Government. In fact, the moot question we need to ask is, are the politicians from the large States empathetic towards the needs of the poor? It is well-known that the rich will foray for themselves, but where the Constituencies are of the less rich, they will bend a sympathetic eye towards the poor. To give an example, in a recent debate about privatization of education held by the *Times Now* television channel, in which brilliant college students and teachers took part, the focus issue was privatization of education. One question asked was, if those living on Rs. 33 a day can be considered as belonging to the above poverty line, where can such families find money for high fees and to pay tutors so that their children can get into private institutions. Or, even if they have the gumption to want to fight to get into private institutions, what promise is there that their children would get into high-paying jobs as to their rich counterparts who are in the same private schools. So, even discussing privatization on a countrywide basis has no meaning unless it is subsidized for a complete population just as is done in Finland. In fact, one of the professors participating in the debate, had very straightly said that there should be complete government subsidy from zero to post-graduate years of education. (Times Now Channel, 28 February, 2012). However, this suggestion seems impractical, for the Government does not have the funds to completely educate all children for all times. Nor it is acceptable to those who can afford to pay to part with some of their money for those 25 per cent students to be admitted in school from the disadvantaged social groups (Indian Express, 25 Feb. 2012). Therefore, our next hypothesis is that there will continue to be only spoken words in favour of the poor, and little follow-up of action validating these spoken words.

We have iterated again and again that the major fulcrum which the poor can hold on to and increase their status thereby is education per se. However, when it is known that they do not even have enough to feed themselves, it is unimaginable to think of an Utopia where the Government will go around paying every born child's fees for education throughout their lives. If this is not a solution when the Government is subsidizing the state schools, what stops it from raising the standards of these schools and maintaining quality education for the poor or at least for the less rich? These are times when there is strict competition for high-paying jobs and therefore there should be some attempt to monitor the quality of education. How can the poor get to that level of quality of education and without the prospect of good jobs in sight. For the major cry of the poor is that even if they finish their education, good-paying jobs are hard to come by since they are usurped by the upper socio-economic classes who also belong to the "upper" castes. With the elections approaching, the politicians are more interested in their own welfare than in the welfare of the poor.

Naturally, the larger States that have more constituencies will have greater chances of their own people to be elected to the Parliament. Unfortunately, they suffer from amnesia in thinking about the greater numbers of poor they have to answer to.

The last hypothesis and probably the strongest is that the large poor States, with large percentage of poor people and probably more constituencies, will more likely have more members representing the poor in the State Assembly. Unfortunately, the same story will prevail. Their issues are not represented by those whom they have elected. They are more concerned with ego-centric issues. The cracks will appear when one of the two major parties are scrabbling to make up the number to form the majority Party and hence, the Government if they stand alone, the majority Party will probably have a greater power than if they have to keep pleasing their coalition partners at all times.

Unless there is transparency of the commitment and the genuineness of those elected in the transferring of money straight from the banks meant for the target group, very little will actually be transformed into better quality infrastructure, more respectable jobs, better health and education facilities.

Since the same will be the same, there is not much hope of state support for such events to happen. Perhaps some expectations of such support by the target group itself will only occur if the monies are handed to them directly for their own better quality livelihood, so that one does not get to hear such absurd dialogue on television, where a farmer tells his wife "I am going to the *Panchayatghar*, because they give us good information from their computers on crops harvesting seasons and farming." When it is well-known, as we have said a few paragraphs above, that globalization and liberalisation having crept into the country, many of the poor farmers are more poor than before and they are less likely to understand computer language.

It is well-known that with sufficiently high GDP, there is more flexibility from the central revenue to assist the poor in different States. However, the Central Government itself has currently a waning economy. Some of the Central revenues accrue to it from State revenues mainly in the form of taxes. It is binding upon all State Governments to contribute to the general exchequer and we assume hypothetically that the contribution is greater from the richer States. With the revenues collected from the States, the Central government plans and budgets for development programmes at the State level.

It is evident that as technology and industrialisation increase, the richer States will need to contribute relatively larger amounts to the Central exchequer. Other things being equal, we might also hypothesise that every individual should get equal distribution of the benefits from the Central revenue if the poor are to improve their status. This does not happen.

As the world shrinks in terms of globalization and technological exchange, the less developed States will leach from the richer States for just sustenance since standards of living even at a minimal level, require greater expenditure than before, especially consumer expenditure. True, India is an emerging country (hastening in development in relation to the developed countries), a time will come when the apportioning of revenues will become problematic between the poor and the rich States. However fast the rich climb up the ladder, there are teeming numbers of poor waiting at the bottom to be able to also climb the ladder. We hypothesise that in time to come the richer States will want to separate from the rest of the States that are poor as they are more developed and probably can compare favourably with developed countries. For example, the malls in the metropolitan areas, the metros, the means of electronic communication and transportation in these metropolises, like Mumbai, Delhi, Calcutta, are almost on par with those existing in some countries in the West. In these medley, the richer States might demand separation, at least in terms of wealth and power and moving away from democracy, social welfare democracy and now what is suggested participatory democracy. They will want their parameters confined to themselves. This is not an unusual trend. Individuals and countries have the same phenomenon. Keeping what they earn to themselves and for themselves and perhaps a kind of a patent balkanization might take place. It is not impossible that this could happen since India conveniently has States with different languages, different sub-cultures, different habits and customs which are heterogeneous and, therefore, they might mark out a place for themselves within the subcontinent of India, where there will possibly be a review and a reassessment of the relationship between state and centre whereby richer States will demand that they be not deprived of the privileges they have earned on their own. In a way, this is probably a knee-jerk for the poorer States who will then not depend so much on *karma* and *dharma* as excuses for their state in life, but will awaken to work in competition with the better-off States.

Given the confused state at the Centre, there is a policy paralysis. Many Bills are still pending and the recent Parliamentary sessions have not been productive. These indicate confusion as to representation at different levels and the breaking away of coalitions, veering towards a hung parliament. The issue really is what determines the strength of the leadership: is it the personality (of the leaders), is it money (black money), is it the known Parties with a profile of transparency or accountability? Or, is it just that the people by and large are looking for change after this tremendously long period of scams. These scams show up Ministers going to jail, coming out on bail, and whistle-blowers being done away surreptitiously. Therefore, is it terror of lawlessness and disorder, spreading from one area to another where ethics and custom mean little to those who are working behind doors to toss over the intentions of the good into the mire. This is akin to the saying that a small number of the good cannot withstand the torrent of evil. Added to this confusion is the upheaval recently caused by a large number of companies relating to the BJP President who is said to own these companies which are not notated.

This scenario of upheaval was clearly evident in the elections to the largest State in the country, Uttar Pradesh, and will continue to show up in the forthcoming batches of State elections where the motto has been and will be "each man for himself". Gone are the days when we could identify a few more Mahatma Gandhis. Now, it is a question of grabbers and grabbing. The tentative hypotheses we have raised above are in relation to the elections for 2014. But, what will happen in the coming elections every five years, what kind of unethical and lack of law and order, will be brought about in the 28 States and 5 Union Territories is something that cannot be reliably predicted. People's facades are changing and unethical methods in the policy are increasing by leaps and bounds.

Even now in this first set of State elections, their plight of the poor has been ignored. In the forthcoming elections we do not envisualise any deviation from the same phenomena, as the same set of politicians will be competing. If the theory of mankind holds good, namely, that everyone works for himself before thinking of others, it cannot be more true than for the Indian politicians who since the last 60 years have not been transparent, committed or promise-keeping.

India has grown from being a social welfare country to a democratic country and now it is being suggested, it should be a participatory democracy since the poor population is too large and they are left out of the participation in the governance of the country. Being a federal government, the central government is required to look after the needs of all in all States irrespective of their relative productivity. The better off States are more or less capable of maintaining stability in revenues and expenditure. But, poor States are crumbling under the weight of high price rise and low revenues. For this reason, large States which have a large proportion of the poor have to look to the Centre for assistance. It is well-known that unless assistance comes in the form of hand-to-hand delivery, there are many other grabbing hands in between to deplete the amounts that are actually meant to be used at the ground level for the target group, namely the poor. By inference, the smaller States even though they may contain a large proportion of the poor are more capable of using their revenue and their proportion of central funds to better take care of their own poor since there is much more cohesion than existing in large states like Rajasthan which is a great fill of desert and infertile land and has poor people with lesser occupational skills. There is already resentment from these small well-to-do states like Punjab and Maharashtra that their taxes are being utilized for the benefit of the poor of the larger States besides their own. As such, we hypothesise that, eventually a time will come when these rich States which are better off will want to utilise their own revenues for their own betterment without sharing and would want to break-away to formulate their own law and order and revenue and expenditure systems. Therefore, the onus is on the large states containing a large proportion of the poor with poor funds and poor budgetary allocations to take care of their own poor people.

If the trend is to continue "things are as is where is" for every election, somewhat the same will happen in the future as said before where the poor will continue to be relatively poor even though the GDP might rise again. It is left to the Central government, therefore, to put more of the allocated revenues into the welfare of the poorer States, especially in the areas of education and health.

Over the last 60 odd years, there seems to be subtle slow-moving factors which at one and the same time raise the status of the rich and correspondingly lower the status of the poor. If at all the poor have done anything to better their status, it is mainly by their own ingenious efforts, either singly or community-wise or with the help of genuine committed NGOs. If the same trend as we are witnessing now will continue, it will go on for several more decades till a muddled confusion occurs and as we have hypothesized before, there will be separation of States into many little counties like the balkanization that happened to the erstwhile Europe and the fragmentation of the USSR into small nations like Uzbekistan, Kazakstan, Azerbaijan, Ukrain, Latvia, Georgia, Lithuania, Moldavia and so on. This probability of balkanization is implied in the great heterogeneity of India, where there are differences in caste, ethnicity, religion, region and social inequalities among them.

The continuation of the old regime will stigmatise the regimes to come, unless the young are more pro-active and are more change-oriented, especially for the benefit of the poorer sections in the country. India is known to be an emerging country in terms of development. But the reality is that the development has not happened where it should, namely, with the poor.

As the years go by, the rich have access to private schooling and education and a greater probability of going abroad and working in other countries as NRIs. This results in their utilization of Indian resources for their education to become professionals but using their professional knowledge and abilities for the benefit of other countries. The children of the poor do not even reach the secondary school level, many do not even reach the primary school level. Worse still, of the 9.7 million children dying globally before they reach the age of five, India accounts for 2.1 million (UNICEF, 2008).

Therefore, where is the incentive given to the poor by the Government, both from the Centre and from the States, to improve their status to have the same and similar advantages of those children born to the rich and now even the upper middle class. For, the situation in India is such that there is no family planning imposition, but only voluntary curtailment of family size. This is not in line with what the poor feel, namely, the more children they have, the greater their security in their old age because there will be more children to take care of them, especially by their sons. The food security bill has not yet been passed. In view of the Millennium Development Goals subscribed to by India, this food security Bill is not a gimmickry as the future health of children in the poorer strata depends upon the implementation of this Bill

(Razia Ismail, 2012). Yet, at the same time, food from outside India will affect, as said before, the production ability of the already stressed small-scale farmers.

Unless there is a government that impose restrictions on themselves and not write tomes and tomes of what they intend to do to help the country, and unless they are willing to themselves see what is happening at the village site, and install the necessary help, these leaders are going to continue to be rhetoric officials who speak without the basic knowledge of what is happening at the ground level in terms of the lives of the poor and the many hurdles they meet with.

The politician's pandora's box reveals that the Supreme Court as far back as in 2002 directed that a person standing as a candidate in an election should disclose whether he has any criminal charge-sheet filed against him at least in the six months before standing for the elections. This, however, as we know, has been ignored in the main as it is easy for criminals to buy tickets for contesting elections so that their future career can be further established for the continuation of their corrupt practices. For instance, of the 337 candidates in the UP Assembly elections held in February-March 2012, about 32 per cent belonging to the parties of SP, BSP, Congress, BJP had serious criminal charges pending against them (Rajindar Sachar, "Whither Indian Politics / Elections?", Mainstream, March 2-8, Vol. L, No. 11, p. 4).

As we write these pages, more and more grist for the mill keeps piling up. There are all kinds of intrigues apparent, now that the incumbent Government of India is faced again and again with comments indicating its ineptitude and inaction. Within the four walls of the United Progressive Alliance, patchwork therapy is being planned. Four senior Cabinet Ministers have offered to resign from their posts. As they put it piously, "We wish to work for the Party." This statement and such like do not fool the public. The former wants to show that they are a loyal force, the Party comes first before the post. There is also some snide remarks that they are probably wanting to appear in high profile in view of the forthcoming 2014 general elections. Somewhere there is a lurking feeling that their pious intentions will be noticed by the High Command and they will be inducted into the Cabinet reshuffle. There is even mention that "we can work under Rahulji's guidance", implying that when he is expected to become the next

Prime Minister, they would be noticed for their loyalty to the Party which is Rahul Gandhi's pet theme, namely, working for the Party at the grassroots level and then they would be in the limelight. Further, after 25 years the Bofors case has been revived and the Chief Investigators who are the whistleblowers are now giving detailed information on how the politicians in 1986 were involved but everything was kept under cover, even mentioning the names of the Gandhi dynasty. This is material upon which the opposition Party, BJP, will now take delight in asking embarrassing questions of the United Progressive Alliance which is maintaining a stoic silence and almost apologizing for not having taken the reform bills over the past two sessions, promising they will now be taken up. The way the members of the UPA appear is that, they are finding it hard to maintain a balance. Some behave as if they lost their caps. Some appear as if they are carved of a stone. Some appear in Parliament with fixed smiles on their faces. And yet others are discussing earnestly ways and means of toppling down the ruling Party.

India appears like a huge lumbering, tottering elephant standing on the brink of a precipice. It looks confused as to which foot to put forward lest it slips, whether it is the right foot or the left foot. It will be pondering while other small elephants are at its back, running towards it in a perilous fashion, while at the foot of the hill are poor farmers trying to till an infertile land and looking up with amusement at he lumbering, stumbling great elephant that is India!

REFERENCES

Government of India, 2001, *Census Abstract, Census of India,* see http://censusindia.gov.in/Census_And_You/age_structure_and_marital_status.aspx

Chatterjee, Srikanta, Allan Rae and Ranjan Ray, 2007, *Food Consumption and Calorie Intake in Contemporary India,* eSocial Sciences Working Paper, Mumbai.

Government of India, 2006, *Agriculture Statistics at a Glance.*

E. Sreedharan and Bharat Wakhlu (eds.), 2012, *Restoring Values: Keys to Integrity, Ethical Behaviour and Good Governance.* Delhi, Sage Publications.

Global March Against Child Labour, 2006, *India Country Report 2006: Review of Child Labour, Education and Poverty Agenda.* New Delhi.

Govt. of India, 2005, *Selected Educational Statistics,* Ministry of Human Resources Development.

Indian Express, 25 February, 2012, "EWS quota: Gurgaon Schools close for a day".

Isaac, 2005, *The Globalization Gap, Pearson Education Inc.*, New Jersey.

Patnaik, Utsa, The Hindu, 15-01-2012, "Poverty, Mass Deprivation Rising in Asia".

Patnaik, Utsa, "Unleashing the market: global capitalism, deflation and agrarian crisis in developing countries", in Mary E. John, Praveen Kumar Jha, Surinder S. Jodhka (eds.), *Contested transformations: changing economies and identities in contemporary India.* Tulika Press: New Delhi.

Planning Commission data quoted in *Review of Child Labour, Education and Poverty Agenda, India Country Report, 2006, by* Global March Against Child Labour, New Delhi, 2006.

Rajindar Sachar, "Whither Indian Politics / Elections?", Mainstream, March 2-8, Vol. L, No. 11, p. 4.

Ravallion, Martin, 2001, "Growth, Inequality and Poverty" Looking Beyond Averages", *Policy Research Working Paper Series, 2558,* The World Bank.

Razia Ismail, "No Guarantee of Food Security in Children's Incredible India", *Mainstream,* March 2-8, 2012, Vol. L, No. 11.

Saurabh Mishra, 2005, "Seeds of Ruin" at Down to Earth: Science and Environment Online, June 15, 2005.

Sengupta, Somini, March 13, 2009, "As Indian Growth Soars, Child Hunger Persists". *The New York Times.* Retrieved 06.11.2011.

Sobhan, Rehman, 2010, *Challenging the Injustice of Poverty: Agendas for Inclusive Development in South Asia,* New Delhi: Age India, pp. 516.

Srinivasan, Rukmini, "No Financial Crisis Impact? India's Poor Grew by 34 million", The Times of India, February 10, 2010.##http://taxguru.in/finance/swiss-bank-revealed-indian-have-more-money-then-rest-of-the-world.html

Times Now Channel debate on 28 February, 2012.

UNICEF, 2009, *The State of the World's Children.* New York: UNICEF.

Yusuf Sayed, Mamya Subramanian, Crain Soundien, Nazir Carrim, *et al., Education Exclusion and Inclusion: Policy and implementation in South Africa and India.* Department of International Development, Researching the Issues, No. 72, 2007.

Index